# COMBAT AIRCRAFT

## 150

# SPITFIRE PHOTO-RECCE UNITS OF WORLD WAR 2

SERIES EDITOR TONY HOLMES

**150**

COMBAT
AIRCRAFT

Andrew Fletcher

# SPITFIRE PHOTO-RECCE UNITS OF WORLD WAR 2

OSPREY
PUBLISHING

OSPREY PUBLISHING
Bloomsbury Publishing Plc
Kemp House, Chawley Park, Cumnor Hill, Oxford OX2 9PH, UK
29 Earlsfort Terrace, Dublin 2, Ireland
1385 Broadway, 5th Floor, New York, NY 10018, USA
E-mail; info@ospreypublishing.com
www.ospreypublishing.com

A catalogue record for this book is available from the British Library.

ISBN; PB 9781472854612; eBook 9781472854629; ePDF 9781472854599;
XML 9781472854605

23 24 25 26 27   10 9 8 7 6 5 4 3 2 1

Edited by Tony Holmes
Cover Artwork by Gareth Hector
Aircraft Profiles by Jim Laurier
Index by Zoe Ross
Typeset by PDQ Digital Media Solutions, UK
Printed and bound in India by Replika Press Private Ltd

Osprey Publishing supports the Woodland Trust, the UK's leading woodland
conservation charity.

To find out more about our authors and books visit www.ospreypublishing.com.
Here you will find extracts, author interviews, details of forthcoming events and
the option to sign up for our newsletter.

**Acknowledgements**
The Author gratefully acknowledges the assistance he has been given by the
following individuals – Peter Arnold, John Bendixsen, Karen Blais, John Blyth,
Peter Brearley, Steve Brooking, Sally Brown, Roy Buchanan, Angus Clark, Michael
Cunliffe-Lister, Marguerite Fewkes, Tim Fryer, Chris Goss, William Hogg, Tony
Hoskins, Roy Kenwright, Dave Lefurgey, Cherry Lenderink, Hans Nauta, Edward
McManus, Stephen Mitchell, Vicky Peterson, Mick Prendergast, Malcolm Ring,
Jimmy Taylor, Tricia Vincent, Dave Wadman, Nick Webb and Bill Williams.

**Front Cover**
On 29 May 1944 Flt Lt G R Crakanthorp of
No 542 Sqn was tasked with covering the
German North Sea ports in Spitfire PR XI
MB791. After refuelling at Coltishall, the
pilot set course for Germany, where he
photographed Bremen, Hamburg and
Wilhelmshaven from 37,000 ft without
incident. As he left the Wilhelmshaven area
he observed what he identified as a Me 163
climbing rapidly at about 3000 ft per
minute. Crakanthorp immediately began to
climb, and as he reached 41,000 ft the
enemy aircraft was only a few thousand
feet below him. As he readied to turn into
the anticipated attack, the exhaust plume
on the Me 163 stopped and it turned away
without gaining further height. He soon lost
sight of his pursuer and set course for
Coltishall to refuel.

Crakanthorp had encountered a Me 163
of *Erprobungskommando* 16, based at Bad
Zwischenahn. The rocket-powered fighter
had commenced combat trials earlier that
month, and this was the first known
instance of a PR Spitfire being intercepted
by the type. It seems likely that the Me 163
ran out of fuel just as the pilot was about to
commence his attack. Although it had a
frighteningly high top speed and rate of
climb, its endurance was very limited.
Fortunately for Crakanthorp, he had been
intercepted west of Wilhelmshaven, so the
Me 163 was operating at the limit of its
endurance and the extra few thousand feet
he gained probably saved him from being
attacked (*Cover artwork by Gareth Hector*)

**PREVIOUS PAGES**
Spitfire PR XI PM151 of Canadian-manned
No 400 Sqn is seen between sorties at Petit
Brogel (B90) during early April 1945. The
PR squadrons directly supporting Allied
armies on the Continent were constantly on
the move as they followed close on the
heels of the advancing troops. Many of their
landing grounds were little more than
muddy fields, but at Petit Brogel the airstrip,
taxiways and dispersals had been
constructed with pierced steel planking.
This was an immediate hit with the pilots,
who found the surface very stable. This in
turn greatly aided taxiing, take-offs and
landings (*Author's Collection*)

# CONTENTS

# INTRODUCTION

ew aircraft have captured the imagination like the Supermarine Spitfire. Designed by Reginald Mitchell to fulfil an Air Ministry specification for a high performance fighter aircraft, the Spitfire entered service with the Royal Air Force (RAF) from August 1938. Serving throughout the conflict, the original design was constantly modified and upgraded, with numerous variants and marks appearing to maintain the type's edge over Axis fighters. One role performed by the Spitfire that is often overlooked is as a photographic-reconnaissance (PR) platform.

Military commanders have always known the value of intelligence. If you are able to ascertain your enemy's intentions through observing his activities and the disposition of his forces, you are always likely to be one step ahead of him, and thus counter his strategies. With the advent of the aeroplane, it was to be expected that military minds would seek ways to utilise this new technology.

The first use of aircraft during World War 1 was for tactical reconnaissance (Tac/R) over the frontlines for the army. Initially, such operations were undertaken by a pilot making observations and reporting what he had seen when he landed. Soon, an observer was added, and it was not long before hand-held cameras were introduced to accurately record what was being seen from the air. As the war progressed, great advances in aircraft and camera technology were made, but photographic operations remained largely tactical in nature, with flights limited to the battle area.

Spitfire I PR Type A N3071 of the Special Survey Flight taxis at Nancy in December 1939. It was one of the first two Spitfires converted for the PR role. Using the principles laid out in the Longbottom Memorandum, N3071 was stripped of excess weight to enable it to climb higher and fly faster, and it also utilised a non-standard camouflage scheme to be less conspicuous at altitude. N3071 carried out the first successful PR Spitfire sortie of the war on 22 November 1939 when Flt Lt Maurice Longbottom photographed Elsenborn, Eupen and Spa from 33,000 ft (*Author's Collection*)

At the end of World War 1 it was clear that aerial reconnaissance had attained a level of importance that at the start of hostilities was unimaginable. In the newly formed RAF, many valuable lessons had been learned in respect to target selection, whilst the quality of the cameras, and the photographs they took, had also greatly improved. Nevertheless, it remained the fact that practically all reconnaissance efforts were in support of the British Army, rather than in the pursuit of independent air operations by the RAF.

In the mid-1930s, as international tensions increased, the RAF's efforts to monitor Italian interests in Africa showed up many shortcomings in how photographic demands were implemented and images obtained. In the years leading up to the outbreak of World War 2, the British Secret Intelligence Service (SIS) had taken an interest in PR as a means of gathering intelligence on Germany. Through liaisons with their French counterparts, three Lockheed 12A twin-engined aircraft were ordered and former World War 1 pilot Frederick S Cotton recruited to carry out covert operations. Under the guise of private company the Aeronautical Research and Sales Corporation, it was planned that Australian Cotton and his Canadian co-pilot Robert H Niven would fly the aircraft around Germany obtaining photographs of military and industrial installations.

From spring 1939 until the end of August, Cotton and Niven flew a series of sorties over Germany, as well as over Italian territories in the Mediterranean and East Africa, where they took numerous photographs of potential targets.

It was during the course of the Italian sorties in June that Cotton and Niven made the acquaintance of Flg Off Maurice V Longbottom, a pilot with No 202 Sqn based at Malta. Longbottom took a keen interest in the methods employed by Cotton and Niven, and accompanied them on one of their sorties. At the end of the month Longbottom returned to Britain and was attached to the Air Ministry in London, where he was involved with the analysis of the photographs obtained on the Italian sorties. Whilst in London Longbottom met frequently with Cotton and Niven, where they discussed at length how to perfect their PR techniques.

With his attachment to the Air Ministry coming to an end, Longbottom submitted a memorandum which formalised the trio's ideas. The document was to prove prescient in that it concluded that in order to obtain photographs from deep within hostile territory, an aircraft would have to operate at great height and speed so as to avoid interception. It duly advocated the use of the most advanced single-engined fighter type then available to the RAF, the Spitfire. These machines would be stripped of all excess weight and have fixed camera installations, increased fuel capacity and a special camouflage scheme to render them less conspicuous at altitude.

Using the principles set out in the Longbottom Memorandum, PR in the RAF during World War 2 evolved from an experimental concept into the primary means of gathering intelligence. As envisioned, the aircraft that proved this concept was the Spitfire, with PR variants of the famous fighter ranging across both Europe and, ultimately, other theatres. Relying on their superior performance, plus the ability of their pilots to avoid detection and interception, they penetrated deep into enemy territory in order to bring back photographs that specialist interpreters could scrutinise to determine the enemy's activities.

Initially formed as an experimental development flight, the Photographic Reconnaissance Unit (PRU) grew from a small clandestine flight of the SIS into an operational group fulfilling the photographic requirements of not just the RAF but many other varied agencies from the Admiralty and War Office to the Ministry of Economic Warfare. As demands for the PRU's services grew, and better versions of the Spitfire became available, new reconnaissance units were formed, both at home and overseas, to meet the ever-growing requirement for aerial intelligence.

Initially limited to operating from Britain, PR Spitfires finally began to be permanently issued to overseas units from 1942. Their superior performance had an immediate impact, with Spitfires operating from Malta and North Africa helping keep watch on German and Italian forces in the Mediterranean. Further afield in Southeast Asia, Spitfires flying over vast tracts of jungle in Burma monitored the movements of Japanese troops.

As the tide of war slowly turned against the Axis powers, and in preparation for the return of Allied armies to German-occupied Europe, an expansion and reorganisation of PR assets took place, with units being allocated to directly fulfil the needs of the forces that would be fighting on the Continent. In parallel with the evolution of the RAF's PR organisation, the Spitfire was gradually improved with the fitment of better cameras and increased range and performance. This latter proved vital, especially for those aircraft operating over Europe, as the Luftwaffe made great efforts to intercept reconnaissance aircraft.

The latest marks of the reconnaissance Spitfire were able to maintain a performance advantage for the most part, even though their pilots were always in great danger. With the appearance of German jet and rocket fighters at the end of 1944, it is notable that Spitfires were far more likely to survive in areas where these types were known to be active compared to other Allied reconnaissance aircraft.

Serving until the very end of the conflict, PR Spitfires allowed the Allies to carefully monitor the activities of the Axis powers and plan the conduct of the war accordingly. The contribution these aircraft, the men that flew them and the organisation behind their operation made to the Allied victory is out of all proportion to the relatively small number of PR Spitfires that were built.

# CHAPTER ONE

# AN EXPERIMENTAL CONCEPT

Flt Lt 'Shorty' Longbottom taxis Spitfire I PR Type A N3071 directly into a hangar at Nancy. The Special Survey Flight relocated here from Coulommiers in early December 1939 in order to be better placed to cover the German frontier. Poor weather initially limited operations, and it was not until 21 December that two successful sorties photographed targets between Bitburg and Saarbrücken (*Author's Collection*)

Shortly after Britain declared war on Germany on 3 September 1939, the Air Ministry approved a plan to develop and expand the SIS Flight under the auspices of the RAF. The excellent results achieved by the flight and the ideas laid out in the Longbottom paper had not gone unnoticed. Formation of a new experimental unit was authorised around the nucleus of the SIS Flight, it being based at Heston aerodrome, then in Middlesex. On 23 September the SIS Flight was formally handed over to the Air Ministry and was henceforth known as the Heston Flight.

During the remainder of September and into October personnel establishment was brought up to strength, with the first two pilots being Niven and Longbottom, although it was 13 October before the first Spitfire (N3069) was received. Modification began immediately, with all guns and armour removed to save weight as well as the wireless and any other unnecessary equipment. The aircraft was camouflaged in 'Camotint', a pale duck egg green. A second example, N3071, arrived a few days later and was likewise modified.

Both aircraft were then sent to the Royal Aircraft Establishment (RAE) for further modification. Here, each side of the sliding canopy hood was fitted with a blister to enable better visibility and a standard F24 camera with a five-inch focal length lens installed vertically in each wing, the cameras being operated by a control unit in the cockpit. Subsequent tests revealed that the top speed had been increased to 390 mph – a significant improvement on the standard fighter. In order to increase the Spitfire's modest radius of operation Cotton had requested that an additional fuel tank be fitted, but no such installation was made on the grounds that it would affect the handling characteristics of the aircraft.

On 1 November the Heston Flight was re-designated No 2 Camouflage Unit in an effort to disguise its true purpose. As the Spitfires lacked the range to reach German targets from Britain, Cotton set about planning operations from France. On 5 November a small detachment, known as the Special Survey Flight, was sent to Lille/Seclin to work directly under the Air Officer Commanding-in-Chief (AOC-in-C) No 1 Air Mission, Air Marshal Sir Arthur Barratt.

On the 20th the flight began a move to a new base at Coulommiers. It was planned that Flt Lt Longbottom would fly the first operational sortie, to cover the German frontier around Aachen, on this date and land at the new airfield. Taking off from Seclin in the morning, Longbottom (in N3071) headed for Germany, where he found his objectives obscured by cloud. With no prospect of the conditions improving, Longbottom returned to France.

On the 22nd Longbottom was again briefed to cover the Aachen area. This time he flew N3071 from Coulommiers to Bar-le-Duc to refuel before heading towards his objectives. Despite haze obscuring targets on the German side of the border, he succeeded in covering Eupen, Elsenborn and Spa, all in neutral Belgium, from 33,000 ft, before landing back at Bar-le-Duc to refuel after a flying time of 1 hr 40 min. Although his photographs were somewhat hazy and their small scale made interpretation of detail difficult, the results were generally satisfactory.

On 5 December the Special Survey Flight relocated to Nancy, but it was to be the 21st before any success was achieved. In a sortie lasting 85 minutes, Flt Lt Niven succeeded in covering targets between Wittlich and Saarbrücken. Within 25 minutes of landing the aircraft was again airborne, this time flown by Longbottom, who photographed Trier, Bitburg and Waxweiler. New Year's Day of 1940 saw Niven succeed in covering targets in the Kaiserslautern area, but he had a lucky escape the following day;

'I spotted fighters over Trier at 25,000 ft so turned south to Saarbrücken, which was reached at 32,000 ft. Started cameras and flew to Kaiserslautern and then along the Rhine to [Bad] Kreuznach. While trying to retrieve my map from the floor I passed out. Regained consciousness at 15,000 ft with aircraft in a spin but unable to regain control until 3000 ft. By this time I had spun over 60 miles out of control and was finally level over Saarbrücken.'

Niven's blackout was caused by his oxygen hose becoming detached when he lent forward to pick up his map, hypoxia quickly causing him to lose consciousness. On the 10th he took off to cover targets in the

Flt Lt Bob Niven climbs into the cockpit of a Camotint Green Spitfire I PR Type B at Heston. He was one of the first two operational pilots of the Heston Flight who, together with Longbottom, proved the concept of high-speed, high-altitude photographic reconnaissance. As the PDU expanded, Niven was responsible for training many of the unit's new pilots (*Author's Collection*)

Saarbrücken area but was intercepted by four Bf 109s near Rohrbach. Niven was chased back to the frontier near Trier before he was finally able to lose his pursuers. This proved to be the last sortie of the Special Survey Flight, for the unit was then ordered to return to Heston.

In a little over two months Spitfire N3071 had undertaken 15 sorties, ten of which had been successful. Poor weather had kept the aircraft grounded for much of the time, but the photographs that were obtained covered targets for the Air Ministry, RAF Bomber Command, the Advanced Air Striking Force (AASF), the Air Component of the British Expeditionary Force (BEF) and extensive coverage of the Siegfried Line for the French.

Although the imagery was small in size, and N3071's limited range restricted the area over which photography could be carried out, the Special Survey Flight had clearly demonstrated what could be achieved. As well as proving the concept of high-speed, high-altitude PR, much valuable operational experience had been gained. Pilots would need to keep a constant watch for contrails forming from their own machines, for they pointed out their exact position to the enemy.

The physiological effects of flying regularly at altitude in an unheated and unpressurised cockpit had also been encountered for the first time, with the extreme cold making even simple actions difficult. A more plentiful supply of oxygen was also needed. The pilot's problems did not end once on the ground, for Niven and Longbottom both frequently experienced drowsiness, joint pains and headaches, especially if flying on consecutive days.

When comparing the results of the Special Survey Flight to those of the existing forces allocated to PR at the outbreak of war, the findings are stark. Since 3 September 1939 the Blenheim IVs of No 2 Group, RAF Bomber Command, had been undertaking PR sorties over northwest Germany. These were soon joined by Blenheim IV squadrons of the Air Component, BEF, which were attempting to cover targets in western Germany. In a period of operations lasting roughly twice as long as those of the Special Survey Flight, seven squadrons of Blenheim IVs only managed to cover approximately half the area of the former and, in the process, lost 17 aircraft. In contrast, one specially modified Spitfire with a much shorter range had achieved some excellent results with a much higher success rate and no losses.

At a conference held at the Air Ministry in January it was concluded that the best way of carrying out strategic reconnaissance was to use a small number of aircraft of the highest possible performance such that enemy fighters were incapable of intercepting them, and that the achievements of the Special Survey Flight warranted further development.

Meanwhile, Cotton had finally persuaded the RAE to allow for an

One of the earliest innovations for PR Spitfires was the incorporation of a teardrop fairing on either side of the sliding canopy hood to give the pilot a better view behind and below. It increased his chances of locating targets from high altitude and helped him with the spotting of intercepting fighters approaching from the rear. The teardrop fairing remained in use with PR Spitfires until the introduction of the bulged Malcolm Hood fitted to the Spitfire PR XI (*Author's Collection*)

increase in Spitfire fuel capacity, which resulted in N3069 having an additional 29-gallon tank installed behind the cockpit. The F24 cameras also had their five-inch lenses replaced with ones of eight-inch focal length, thereby greatly increasing the scale of the images produced. Finally, the armoured windscreen was removed in an effort to save further weight. These modifications addressed two of the main lessons learned from operating in France, namely the small scale of the photographs produced and the limited radius of action – the additional fuel increased the maximum range to 750 miles. The new variant was christened the PR Type B, with the previous version retrospectively labelled the Type A.

## PDU

On 17 January 1940, No 2 Camouflage Unit became the Photographic Development Unit (PDU). Remaining experimental in nature, it was realised that much work would be necessary before the unit could be increased in size to fulfil all of the RAF's strategic PR needs, but from this time onwards expansion was rapid. The increased range of the Type B meant that efforts could now be made to cover German targets directly from Britain. Such operations would still entail refuelling at a forward base, but it brought the prospect of regular coverage of the German North Sea ports for the Admiralty.

In addition, the War Office had an urgent task in support of the BEF, where coverage of Belgium was required for the update of maps. Flt Lt Niven duly flew N3071 over to Lille/Seclin on the 18th in preparation for the required survey. The next day he attempted to obtain a mosaic of central Belgium, only to find most of his objectives obscured by cloud. He did, however, succeed in covering eastern sections of the country.

During January the operational element at Heston became known as 'N' Flight and the detachment on the Continent as the PDU (Overseas).

On 10 February Longbottom set off for Wilhelmshaven in N3069 after refuelling at Debden. He made two runs over the port before photographing Schillig Roads, Wangerooge and Emden. With all objectives covered, he set course for home, landing back at Heston 3 hr 20 min after leaving Debden. Not only was this the first successful Spitfire PR sortie undertaken from Britain, it was also the longest in duration.

Another significant event to occur on the 10th was the authorisation of a new establishment which expanded the size of the organisation based in France. To be known as No 212 Sqn, it called for three operational flights of two Spitfires. Although the new unit would be subject to the operational control of AOC-in-C British Air Forces in France (BAFF), it was still very much a part of the PDU.

That same day Flt Lts Niven (N3117) and L E Clark (N3071) flew to Seclin, where they were joined by Flg Off C D Milne and Flt Lt H C MacPhail, the latter being given command of the squadron by Cotton. On the 12th, Clark (N3071) successfully carried out the new squadron's first operational sortie when he covered objectives in central Belgium. At this stage the unit was still very much short of aircraft and pilots but best efforts were made to complete the survey of Belgium. Two successful

A split pair of F24 cameras in a Spitfire I PR Type C. Located in the starboard wing, each camera was equipped with an eight-inch focal length lens and slightly offset from the vertical, one to port and one to starboard, in order to produce a wider field of view to cover a greater area. The Type C was also the first variant to introduce a long focal length camera in the rear fuselage (*Author's Collection*)

sorties were flown the next day, but all three attempted on the 14th were unsuccessful. After this the weather deteriorated, stopping operations until the start of March.

At Heston, the PDU was under pressure for more coverage of the German ports, although the poor conditions made opportunities for photography rare. On 24 February Niven flew Spitfire N3116 on its first operational sortie, having been tasked with obtaining photographs of industrial installations at Duisburg for RAF Bomber Command. Again, cloud forced him to abandon the sortie.

As the PDU and its overseas offshoot, No 212 Sqn, began to grow in size, the need arose for a senior officer to act as Cotton's second in command. As his first deputy MacPhail had been appointed to command No 212 Sqn in France, it was desirable that an officer be appointed to control operations from Heston. At the end of February Sqn Ldr Geoffrey Tuttle was appointed to the position.

On 2 March Niven (N3116) successfully covered targets in the Ruhr. These photographs, which were the first of the area taken during wartime, proved to be of excellent quality and were used extensively to update RAF Bomber Command target dossiers. A second successful sortie was flown from Heston, with new pilot Flt Lt E C Le Mesurier (N3069) obtaining photographs of Emden and Wilhelmshaven. Poor weather then reduced operational flying, although training sorties from Heston were still able to continue. This allowed Flg Offs S L Ring, C M Wheatley and I G Richmond, all of whom were former Battle pilots from the AASF in France, to convert onto the Spitfire.

Of more significance was the delivery of Spitfire P9308. This machine was the latest variant of PR Spitfire, designated the PR Type C. Through the fitment of an extra 30-gallon fuel tank in a bulged fairing beneath the port wing, the aircraft's maximum range had been increased to 1100 miles, with a safe range of about 900 miles. To act as a counterweight to the tank, the two F24 cameras were moved to a fairing under the starboard wing. To allow for the extra flying time permitted by the increased fuel, additional oxygen was carried and an extra large oil tank was installed in the nose. The latter required the fitting of a deeper engine cowling to enclose the tank.

It was also proposed to fit the PR Type C with a vertical camera with a long focal length lens in the rear fuselage. However, for this to be accommodated, the run for the flying control linkages needed to be altered. Due to the urgent operational need for greater range, this modification was not initially incorporated in P9308, although the vertical camera would soon become standard in the PR Type C.

On 16 March No 212 Sqn received a directive from HQ BAFF with a requirement for coverage of the Rhine between the Dutch frontier and Düsseldorf to look for evidence of troop concentrations in advance of an invasion, but numerous sorties were all unsuccessful due to the conditions. Two flights were made from Heston on the 22nd, however, with Flt Lt Le Mesurier using P9308 to complete the first operational sortie undertaken in a Type C. Tasked with obtaining damage assessment (D/A) photographs of the airfield and seaplane base at Sylt, he ultimately had to abandon his effort due to cloud. Although the sortie was unsuccessful, it was the longest in duration and distance yet undertaken, with no refuelling stop being necessary.

No 212 Sqn's Flg Off Ian Richmond is seen in conversation with Wg Cdr Sidney Cotton (right). On 29 March 1940, Richmond (in Type B N3117) was tasked with covering targets in eastern Belgium, but after observing approaching contrails he aborted his flight. Whilst attempting to return to Lille/Seclin, he had difficulty pin-pointing his position and, running low on fuel, attempted to land at Laval. However, his aircraft hit soft ground and nosed over. Damage to N3117 was minimal, but Cotton was not impressed and within days Richmond had been posted back to one of the AASF's Battle squadrons (*Author's Collection*)

Whilst Le Mesurier was airborne, Flg Off Wheatley was refuelling N3069, the first Type B, at Stradishall in West Suffolk, from where he was airborne at 1115 hrs. His objective on this day was the River Rhine from the Dutch frontier to the Ruhr. However, as he crossed into Germany at 33,000 ft near Kleve his aircraft was making heavy contrails. Two Bf 109E-1s were scrambled from the nearby airfield at Bönninghardt to intercept. Although one fighter struggled to reach Wheatley's altitude, the other was just able to get level with the Spitfire. Unable to match its speed, the pilot opened fire at long range. The Spitfire immediately went into a steep dive and was followed down by the Bf 109. At about 16,000 ft Wheatley bailed out, but his parachute did not open and his body fell on the German side of the border.

Flg Off Claude Mervyn Wheatley was the first pilot to be killed flying a PR Spitfire on operations. The circumstances of his loss show the difficulties experienced by the Germans in trying to intercept a fast-moving aircraft at great altitude, but also the dangers posed by contrail formation which negated one of the main advantages that a high-flying Spitfire relied on – stealth.

On 28 March Le Mesurier set another duration record in P9308. In a flight lasting 3 hr 45 min, he carried out the first successful sortie in a Type C when he photographed Cuxhaven from 32,000 ft. As he attempted to cover Wilhelmshaven, he observed a flight of fighters in a tight spiral climb. Not wanting to risk interception, Le Mesurier aborted his run over the port. Three sorties were flown from Seclin the next day. Two were abandoned due to cloud, and Flg Off Richmond (N3117), who was attempting to cover eastern Belgium, observed a contrail approaching when he was southwest of Liège and aborted his flight. Running low on fuel, he landed at Laval, but at the end of his landing run the aircraft hit soft ground and nosed over. Richmond was not hurt and the damage to N3117 was minimal.

This also proved to be the last sortie flown in connection with the Belgium survey. The photographs previously obtained allowed an almost complete mosaic of the whole country to be constructed, facilitating the preparation of new maps. The flight at Seclin could now concentrate on trying to cover the Rhine, the task being extended to include another section of the river stretching to Mainz. It was notable during this period that the Luftwaffe had intensified its efforts to intercept the high-flying Spitfires, but provided a pilot was careful not to produce contrails and kept a keen lookout, he could usually avoid interception.

An increase in aircraft and pilots enabled No 212 Sqn to form a second operational flight at this time. Known as 'B' Flight, it was to operate from Nancy, with the flight at Seclin henceforth known as 'A' Flight. 'B' Flight was initially tasked with covering targets in southwestern Germany, and it was able to carry out two successful sorties on 7 April. Flt Lt Clark covered sections of the River Rhine and River Main and Flg Off A L Taylor photographed the Rhine from Speyer to Sandhofen.

A brief lull in flying at Heston enabled the modification of P9308 to be completed with the installation of a rear vertical camera in the guise of an Eagle IV with a 21-inch focal length lens. The latter would produce images of a much larger scale. On 6 April Flt Lt Le Mesurier (P9308) was tasked with covering Wilhelmshaven. Although conditions were hazy, he was able to take photographs of Emden and Wilhelmshaven that included 61 exposures with the Eagle IV.

The next day Longbottom (P9308) attempted to cover Kiel. As he began his run down the Kieler Förde the starboard-inclined F24 and Eagle IV cameras failed. Fortunately, the other F24 continued to work, and he was able to cover Kiel and the Kaiser Wilhelm Canal. As he approached the end of the canal at Brunsbüttel, he sighted an enemy aircraft only 1000 ft below him. He immediately accelerated, with the enemy aircraft giving chase, but contact was lost near Heligoland and he was able to fly home, setting a new duration record of 3 hr 50 min in the process.

Analysis of Longbottom's photographs revealed a large number of naval and merchant vessels in the port and roadstead. Likewise, images of the airfield at Holtenau showed numerous aircraft, many of them transports or bombers. It was not known at the time, but the high concentration of shipping and aircraft presaged the invasion of Denmark and Norway only two days later. On 11 April No 212 Sqn's 'A' Flight moved to Meaux/Villenoy, where its activities would continue to be focused on the Rhine and the

No 212 Sqn personnel work on the port F24 camera of a Spitfire I PR Type B in France. The Type B introduced lenses of up to eight inches in focal length. In order to accommodate the longer lenses in the wing it was necessary to house the installation in a bulged fairing. Cpl Rawlinson (right) was known as the 'camera wizard' due to his technical prowess (*Author's Collection*)

zone between the Ruhr and the Dutch border. Pilots were looking for any activity indicating preparation for an invasion.

On the 12th, No 212 Sqn and its parent unit the PDU had new establishments approved. 'N' Flight at Heston, which to date had been operating a single Spitfire with only two pilots, was increased to ten pilots and eight Spitfires. No 212 Sqn was scaled for four pilots and three Spitfires for each of its flights.

The activities of 'B' Flight at Nancy were curtailed by the weather, and it was not until 19 April that further successful sorties were flown when Clark covered the Mannheim area and Milne photographed Karlsruhe and the Rhine. The 21st saw Milne (N3116) make an attempt at the Brenner Pass, but poor weather prevented coverage of the objective. In a sortie lasting three hours, he did manage to cover Friedrichshafen, however.

On his second sortie of the day Milne (N3071) attempted to cover sections of the Neckar, Main and Danube. Whilst carrying out a run along the River Neckar southeast of Stuttgart, he failed to notice his aircraft was producing a contrail that allowed two Bf 109s to creep up from behind. The initial bounce damaged Milne's engine, and although he tried to make for the French border he was repeatedly attacked until his engine stopped. He succeeded in bailing out and was immediately captured. N3071 was the original Type A that had made the first ever successful reconnaissance sortie by a Spitfire back in November 1939, although it had since been upgraded to Type B standard.

At the very end of April No 212 Sqn was able to form its third flight. 'C' Flight would be based at Lille/Seclin, where it was tasked with trying to obtain additional cover of Belgian targets. 'C' Flight flew its first sortie on 2 May, when Flg Off S G Wise (P9307) attempted to cover eastern Belgium but thick cloud obscured his target area.

Eight days later the Germans launched their long anticipated attack in the West. However, the main thrust was not across the Belgian Plain as expected but further south through the Ardennes region. The build up of German forces had escaped detection by the French, whose strategic reconnaissance assets were responsible for coverage of the area. Like the conventional units of the RAF, the aircraft used by the *Armée de l'Air* were unable to successfully discharge this duty.

As previously planned, the BEF, as part of the French 1st Army Group, advanced into Belgium not yet aware that the main German threat lay to their south. With news of the German attack, No 212 Sqn's outlying flights at Lille/Seclin and Nancy were recalled to Meaux/Villenoy. Three sorties were flown from Meaux on the 10th aimed at covering enemy troop movements in northeastern Belgium. In the morning, Flg Off A J Blackwell (P9331) and Flt Lt L D Wilson (P9396) successfully covered the area between Mézières and Liège, with Blackwell avoiding the attention of two Bf 109s. In the afternoon Flg Off Taylor succeeded in taking photographs of Mézières, Bastogne, Herenthals and Brussels.

By 14 May it had become evident that the German advance through the Ardennes between Namur and Sedan was threatening to drive a wedge between the French 1st and 2nd Army Groups, and thus unhinge the whole Allied line in northern France.

Although the German advance fell within the area of responsibility of the French HQ, BAFF was well aware of the inability of the *Armée de l'Air* to obtain aerial photographs of the frontline. Given the gravity of the situation, it began to despatch sorties to the area, with the first flown that day when future ace Flg Off G P Christie succeeded in photographing Namur and the Meuse bridges to Liège and Maastricht. Later that morning Taylor successfully carried out a D/A sortie to the area west of the Ruhr following an attack by RAF Bomber Command on communication centres aimed at disrupting German reinforcements. On 21 May Christie did a run along the River Oise between Chauny and Guise and the River Sambre at Landrecies to ascertain the condition of the bridges that had been attacked the previous night by RAF bombers. His initial run was carried out at 31,000 ft, but on the return leg he dropped down to 9000 ft to obtain larger-scale images of the bridges, many of which were still intact.

For the British, the evacuation of the BEF from the Channel ports now became top priority. Flg Off Taylor flew a very successful sortie on the last day of the month when he photographed more than 60 bridges on the River Meuse between Givet and Sedan. Analysis of his photographs showed that although 28 had been destroyed, there were a further 34 intact or only lightly damaged. Five sorties were flown from Meaux on 4 June, of which four were successful. All were connected with covering targets associated with the German advance in France except for the sortie flown by Taylor, who covered the Saarbrücken area and the Rhine between Mainz and Karlsruhe.

With the surrender of the last Allied troops at Dunkirk on the 4th, the Germans turned their attentions to the remainder of France, with No 212 Sqn continuing to be tasked with mostly tactical targets. On the 6th Taylor photographed the Somme between Abbeville and Amiens before covering Péronne and Chauny. Flying P9385, he had taken off from Heston and after photographing his objectives landed at Meaux.

At the request of the French HQ, BAFF tasked No 212 Sqn with covering the railway lines from Aulnoye to Maastricht and up to Venlo which formed the main German supply route across Belgium and into France. Two sorties were attempted on the 7th to fulfil this requirement. The first was undertaken by Flt Lt Wilson (P9331), who successfully covered Aulnoye, Charleroi and Liège, but after the latter his cameras ran away and he returned to Meaux.

Later in the afternoon Flg Off Blackwell, in the same aircraft, attempted to cover the remaining target areas. After climbing to 30,000 ft he crossed into Belgium on course for Liège, and whilst navigating, his map slipped and in his efforts to pick it up Blackwell detached his oxygen supply and quickly passed out. Regaining consciousness at 8000 ft, and unable to pin-point his position, he flew south. Running short on fuel, and with his engine temperature rising due to a coolant leak, Blackwell was forced to land at Rheims/Champagne despite the French having placed obstructions on the airfield. Skilfully landing between the obstacles, the pilot had to abandon his aircraft as it could not be immediately repaired.

Efforts to get P9331 airworthy were unsuccessful, with the RAF eventually requesting that the French destroy the aircraft to avoid it falling into German hands. Sadly, this is exactly what happened, with P9331 being captured intact when the enemy captured the airfield.

9 June saw No 212 Sqn forced to evacuate Meaux as the advancing German troops threatened to cross the Seine west of Paris. No operational sorties were flown that day, as the unit moved to its new base at Orléans/Bricy. On the 10th, future ace Flt Lt J A Kent flew the first sortie from Bricy when he successfully covered the River Seine between Rouen and Mantes-la-Jolie. By the 14th the Germans were only 20 miles west of Orléans, so orders were given to withdraw to Poitiers.

Taylor carried out the last operational sortie by No 212 Sqn from northern France when he made a low-level attempt at covering the Seine and Eure. His aircraft, P9453, was a hybrid which had been modified to carry a split pair of F24 cameras with eight-inch lenses in the rear fuselage along with a 29-gallon fuel tank, although the Spitfire was unique in that it retained the eight 0.303-inch Browning machine guns of the standard fighter. His photographs showed that although many road and rail bridges had been destroyed, a number were still intact, and that the Germans were busy building new ones. His photographic run completed, Taylor headed north and landed at Heston.

The remnants of No 212 Sqn only remained at Poitiers for 48 hours before ultimately moving to La Rochelle, from where the last of the personnel were evacuated back to Britain and the squadron disbanded.

Future ace Flt Lt Johnny Kent climbs into the cockpit of a PR Spitfire at Heston in June 1940. He was one of a small number of early recruits to the PDU whose background was on fighters. It was found that in general fighter pilots lacked the navigational abilities and temperament to make good PR pilots. Kent, who was an experienced pre-war aviator and test pilot, proved to be the exception to the rule, flying a number of successful sorties with the PDU/No 212 Sqn before returning to fighter operations with Polish-manned No 303 Sqn in late July 1940 (*Author's Collection*)

## PDU OPERATIONS

For the PDU at Heston, the German invasion of France and the Low Countries would mean an extension of the coastline they would have to cover. The operations of 'N' Flight would continue to be focused on the German North Sea ports, and to this would be added coverage of the Dutch Frisian Islands and ports which the Admiralty feared would now be used as forward bases by the Kriegsmarine. On 19 May 'N' Flight carried out five such sorties, with four successfully obtaining photographs of numerous targets in Germany and the Netherlands. However, the PDU also suffered its second Spitfire loss of the war when Plt Off J H Coleman (P9308) failed to return from his attempt to cover Hamburg and Bremen, his aircraft, the original Type C, crashing at Templeuve, in Belgium.

Developments on the Continent now resulted in 'N' Flight also being tasked with flying sorties to France in support of the BEF, which was falling back to the Channel ports. With the situation in France rapidly deteriorating, the evacuation of the BEF began on the 27th. For the next nine days 'N' Flight's activities would for the most part be focused on trying to cover enemy troop movements and positions, as well as airfields

Spitfire I PR Type C P9385 was delivered to the PDU in the spring of 1940 and used on both deployments of 'D' Flight No 212 Sqn to southern France for the coverage of Italian targets. It remained on operations with No 1 PRU until November 1941 when the aircraft was relegated to a training role (*Author's Collection*)

and ports that could be utilised by the Germans to launch attacks on the vessels trying to ferry Allied troops back to Britain.

Once Dunkirk had fallen, operations flown from Heston returned to those of a mainly strategic nature, with a period of good weather allowing a number of successful high-altitude missions to be undertaken. On 5 June Flg Off Ring covered ports and airfields in northwest Germany from 32,500 ft. His photographs showed the German capital ships *Tirpitz* and *Admiral Scheer* present at Wilhelmshaven. On the same day Flt Lt P Corbishley covered most of the ports and airfields along the coast from Calais to Zeebrugge, before photographing Antwerp and then returning home.

As No 212 Sqn was occupied with the German assault on the Low Countries and northern France, a newly formed detachment from the squadron prepared to commence operations against Italy. Early in 1940 the Air Ministry had concluded that in the likely event that Italy was to enter the war on the side of Germany, it would be necessary to attack key strategic targets including naval bases and the industrial centres of the north. It was intended that aircraft based in the south of France would commence operations once Italy entered the war. For this force to be able to act immediately it was imperative that up to date target information be available, and it was for this purpose that 'D' Flight of No 212 Sqn was formed.

As Italy was technically still neutral, great care would have to be taken not to draw attention to any operations conducted in the gathering of aerial intelligence. Like the Belgian survey carried out in March, the high-speed, high-altitude PR techniques of the PDU/No 212 Sqn offered the best chance of success.

On 11 May Flt Lt Longbottom flew down to Le Luc, in the south of France, which had been chosen due to its proximity to the Royal Navy detachment at Hyères, where film processing facilities were available. On the morning of the 12th Longbottom carried out the first sortie by 'D' Flight when he successfully covered the Franco-Italian frontier and the ports in the western half of the Gulf of Genoa.

Due to the progress of the German attack in the Low Countries it was decided to recall 'D' Flight, but before leaving two more successful sorties were flown. On the morning of the 14th Flt Lt Le Mesurier (P9308) covered numerous targets in the Milan and Como areas before landing at Bastia, on the island of Corsica. From here, Longbottom flew across Italy, where he photographed Bari, on the Adriatic coast. The next day, Longbottom and Le Mesurier flew back to Meaux and then on to Heston. In just three days they had flown seven successful sorties and covered the most likely routes of advance by the *Regio Esercito* into France, the two big industrial centres of Milan and Turin, most of the ports in the Gulf of Genoa and the port of Bari and its oil refineries.

As the situation in northern France was reaching a critical juncture, and it was increasingly likely that Italy was about to enter the war, the Air Ministry ordered a resumption of the Italian sorties. On 27 May Le Mesurier landed at Le Luc in P9385, a new Type C Spitfire. The next day he carried out the first sortie of 'D' Flight's second deployment when he covered Genoa and Le Spezia. Over the course of the next nine days Le Mesurier and Flg Off D F B Sheen (another future ace) flew ten successful sorties covering all of their objectives in northern Italy. 'D' Flight began operating from Ajaccio, on Corsica, from 8 June in order to cover objectives in the south of Italy.

On the 10th, Italy declared war on Britain and France, and it was thought prudent to withdraw 'D' Flight back to the French mainland. On the 15th Sheen carried out the last sortie of the detachment when he successfully photographed La Spezia, Pisa, Genoa and Savona. With the French in general retreat in the north of the country, 'D' Flight was recalled back to Britain. During the second deployment to the south of France 'D' Flight flew 22 sorties, of which 20 were successful, with all primary objectives being covered at least once.

The achievements of the PDU and No 212 Sqn during the period from the start of the German offensive against the Low Countries up to the withdrawal of No 212 Sqn from France were out of all proportion to the resources employed. During a 40-day period with only a handful of serviceable Type B/C Spitfires, 120 operational sorties were flown, of which 95 were successful. For the loss of only two aircraft and one pilot, target information was gathered on German and Italian ports and industrial sites and tactical information collected on behalf of Allied forces fighting on the Continent.

Although excellent results had been achieved against strategic objectives, this was not always the case with tactical targets. Great efforts were made to photograph troop movements and positions, even though this type of work was not well suited to high-altitude reconnaissance. Towards the end of the campaign a number of sorties were conducted at low-level in order to obtain large-scale photographs. Although these operations exposed pilots to greater risk, such was the urgency of the task that any potential danger was offset by the increased chances of success. Using this method a number of very successful sorties were flown.

# CHAPTER TWO

# EARLY OPERATIONS

Following the disbandment of No 212 Sqn after its withdrawal from France, two new flights were formed within the PDU for detached operations. At the start of July 1940 'A' Flight began operations from Wick and 'B' Flight from St Eval. Spitfire I PR Type C P9550 'LY 19' was assigned to 'A' Flight and flew its first successful sortie on 4 July when cover of Stavanger was obtained (*Chris Goss Collection*)

With the withdrawal of No 212 Sqn back to Heston and its disbandment on 18 June, the Air Ministry took the opportunity to make the PDU a regular operational unit. Although much development work was still being undertaken at this point, the basic concept of high-altitude, high-speed PR had been proven, and it was felt that the time was right to move direct control away from the Air Ministry. Therefore, also on 18 June, operational control of the PDU was passed to RAF Coastal Command.

The Combined Intelligence Committee (CIC), which had been formed at the end of May 1940 to control all aspects of intelligence relating to the threat of German invasion, was responsible for assessing all requests for PR and passing them on to RAF Coastal Command for execution.

On 18 June Wg Cdr Cotton was relieved of his command following numerous clashes with senior officials in the Air Ministry, his place being taken by Wg Cdr Tuttle. Ten days later, another technical development with the Spitfire saw the PDU employ the F8 camera operationally for the first time when Flg Off Taylor covered Rotterdam and Amsterdam in P9382 – a Type C fitted with a single F8 and 20-inch lens combination.

At the end of June two new flights were formed for operations from St Eval, in Cornwall and Wick, in Scotland, these geographically dispersed locations allowing for wider coverage of enemy territory. On 8 July a new establishment was approved, and with it the PDU was re-designated the PRU, with each operational flight established for four aircraft and eight pilots.

In addition, an experimental flight of five Spitfires carried out various trials and was heavily involved in testing a number of camouflage schemes. During earlier operations over the Continent, a blue/grey scheme had been found to be superior to Camotint Green at high altitude, and it was a variation of this colour that ultimately became the standard for PR aircraft.

On 25 July 'E' Flight was formed, but not as a fifth operational flight as originally planned but by renaming the experimental flight. One of the Spitfires in 'E' Flight's inventory was the newly arrived P9384, the first Type F. This variant retained the enlarged oil tank under the chin and carried 89 gallons of additional fuel in single 30-gallon fuel tanks in bulged fairings beneath each wing and a 29-gallon tank behind the pilot, allowing for a safe range of 1100 miles. The camera arrangement consisted of a vertical split pair of F24s or a single F8 in the rear fuselage. Provision was also made for the installation of a port-facing F24 oblique camera for lateral photography.

Two other variants that were part of 'E' Flight were the Types E and G. The former was a unique modification to try and solve the problem of low-altitude photography, with N3117 carrying single F24 cameras installed in fairings beneath each wing, with the cameras aligned perpendicular to the line of flight. This installation used lenses of only 3¼-inch focal length, as space in the wing fairings was very limited. Despite proving that it could bring back good oblique images, the Type E was not a success because it was considered too vulnerable to interception.

Experience with N3117 led to the specification for the Type G, which was fitted with two vertical F24 cameras in the rear fuselage and an oblique F24 camera that could be configured to face either port or starboard. It also had canopy blisters, a 29-gallon fuel tank behind the pilot that gave a safe range of about 750 miles, and retained eight 0.303-inch Browning machine guns and the armoured windscreen of the Spitfire IA. Finally, the aircraft was painted in a very pale green camouflage scheme overall. It was envisioned that the Type G would approach its objectives in or near cloud before descending for photography. The green camouflage scheme was in reality little more than on off-white colour that had been found to offer the lowest contrast against cloud below 15,000 ft.

The modest range of the Type G limited operations to shallow penetrations, and low-level sorties soon

Flt Lt Leonard Clark commanded 'B' Flight No 1 PRU from its formation in July 1940 until he was posted away six months later. He is seen here after 'B' Flight was rotated back to Heston, its place at St Eval having been taken by 'D' Flight. Clark is stood in front of a Type G used for 'dicing', and it is unclear whether the aircraft is camouflaged in Camotint Green or the even paler off-white scheme introduced for low-level operations (*Author's Collection*)

earned a reputation for being even more dangerous than regular PR sorties, with pilots literally dicing with death on a regular basis. This resulted in the Type Gs being infamously dubbed 'dicers'.

On 29 July the Type F made its operational debut when Flt Lt Ring (P9384) successfully covered the Scheldt Estuary. Operations continued apace the following month, with a careful watch maintained on enemy ports and airfields. In the two months the unit had been on invasion watch, photographs did not reveal any appreciable evidence that would suggest preparation for a large-scale seaborne operation. However, by the start of September the increased movement of barges was detected in Dutch and Belgian canals, with vessels all heading towards the Channel ports. In addition, numerous small convoys of merchant vessels were photographed moving down the coast. The build-up in shipping indicated that the Germans appeared ready to commence invasion operations.

On 23 September eight successful sorties were flown which covered every major port between Emden and Brest. The images taken on that day seemed to suggest that a peak had been reached in the numbers of invasion vessels deployed, and sorties flown over the remainder of the month showed a decrease as barges and merchantmen were slowly dispersed. The CIC concluded that the Luftwaffe's inability to achieve air superiority over southern England had likely resulted in a postponement of any invasion attempt during 1940.

At the end of September the PRU received the first prototype Spitfire I PR Type D. P9551 had specially fabricated wing leading edge fuel tanks, each holding 57.5 gallons. The prototype retained the 29-gallon tank behind the pilot, which together with the main fuselage tanks gave a total fuel capacity of 229 gallons, allowing a safe operational range of 1500 miles. As with previous PR variants, the Type D was fitted with teardrop canopy fairings, carried additional oxygen and had an increased oil capacity, but rather than the tank being fitted under the engine it was located in the port wing. Initial camera installation was a split pair of vertical F24s with 14-inch lenses in the rear fuselage.

By October the majority of the PRU's Spitfires had been camouflaged overall 'PRU Blue'. This colour, a mixture of Prussian and cerulean blue, consistently proved the most effective at high altitude.

On 29 October Flg Off S J Millen took off from Heston in P9551, with Berlin as his primary objective. Upon arriving over the German capital, he found it completely obscured by cloud, so he set course for his secondary objectives on the Baltic coast, where he photographed Stettin, Swinemünde and Rostock from 27,000 ft. As well as being the first time many of the targets had been covered, the 5 hr 30 min flight was also a duration record for a PR Spitfire sortie.

## NEW PRU

Although the immediate threat of invasion had passed, much of the PRU's attention was still occupied with the enemy's preparations for an amphibious attack on Britain. This led RAF Bomber Command to voice concerns that its reconnaissance requirements were being neglected in favour of the Admiralty and RAF Coastal Command. It successfully

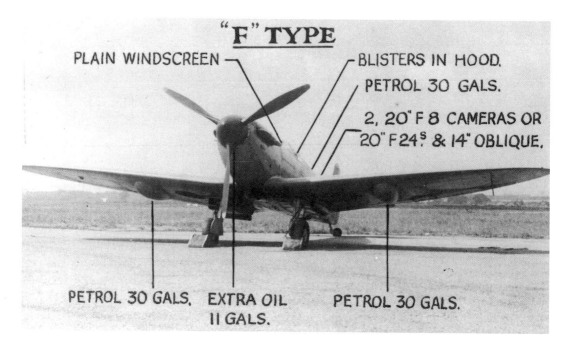

# "F" TYPE

PLAIN WINDSCREEN — ┌ BLISTERS IN HOOD.
PETROL 30 GALS.

2, 20" F 8 CAMERAS OR
20" F 24$^s$ & 14" OBLIQUE.

PETROL 30 GALS.  EXTRA OIL  PETROL 30 GALS.
II GALS.

presented the case for its own PRU, the new unit receiving its tasking directly from HQ RAF Bomber Command and being responsible for obtaining bomb D/A and targeting information. The original PRU was to remain under the operational control of RAF Coastal Command, and it was still required to fulfil the demands of the CIC and all other external agencies.

The date chosen for the reorganisation to take place was 16 November 1940, with the PRU simply being re-designated No 1 PRU. No 3 PRU was also formed on this date for RAF Bomber Command, with a provisional establishment of 12 pilots and four Type C and two Type F Spitfires for daytime operations from Oakington, in Cambridgeshire. No 3 PRU carried out its first sortie on the 29th when its CO, Sqn Ldr P B B Ogilvie (Type C X4385), successfully covered Cologne.

On 17 December, No 3 PRU received another Type C (X4383) from Heston, but unlike in previous machines, its F8 camera was fitted with a 75 cm (29½-inch) lens recovered from a downed German reconnaissance aircraft. The combination produced a hybrid with a focal length far in excess of anything then available to the RAF. It was first used successfully on the 21st, when Flt Lt H C Marshall (X4383) was tasked with covering Cologne.

Finally, on 14 March 1941, Sqn Ldr Ogilvie (Type F X4712) successfully covered Berlin for the first time. In a sortie lasting 4 hr 20 min, he brought back 95 large-scale exposures of the German capital.

## COVERING THE KRIEGSMARINE

Whilst No 3 PRU was working itself up to fulfil the requirements of RAF Bomber Command, the newly named No 1 PRU continued to fulfil it primary role of anti-invasion reconnaissance for the CIC. The Kriegsmarine was now firmly committed to severing Britain's vital sea

This annotated photograph of a Spitfire I PR Type F at Benson in 1941 shows the various modifications incorporated into the variant. Due to delays in the fabrication of the leading edge wing tanks of the Type D, the Type F actually entered service before the former. Many Type Cs were upgraded to Type F standard, although the variant was ultimately superseded by the Type D once it began arriving in numbers during the summer of 1941 (*Author's Collection*) lanes, and it planned to do this by vastly increasing the size of its U-boat force. No 1 PRU would be called upon to monitor the progress of this new and expanding threat.

On 26 December 1940, No 1 PRU moved to Benson, in South Oxfordshire, although the landing area at the new airfield became very soft with the winter rains and operations were soon undertaken from the satellite at Mount Farm, which had paved runways.

1940 had been a year of rapid development for the PRU, seeing it increase in size from a small experimental unit equipped with two Spitfires into the primary means of gathering strategic photographic intelligence for all three services. For the year as a whole, the PRU in all its guises had flown well over 1000 Spitfire sorties, of which more than 80 per cent were successful.

Since 27 December the German heavy cruiser *Admiral Hipper* had been at Brest after sortieing into the Atlantic. It was not until 9 January 1941 that aircraft flying from St Eval were able to secure clear images of the vessel when Flg Off P H Watts made a low-level run across the Rade-de-Brest. In the months to come, Brest would be constantly photographed to monitor naval activity at the port.

At Benson, long on the list of tasks outstanding was a requirement by the Admiralty for coverage of the Italian fleet at La Spezia and Genoa. The only aircraft with the capability to safely make such a deep penetration was a Type D Spitfire. On 19 January, Flt Lt Corbishley (P9551) was tasked with covering the ports. Due to cloud and a strong tailwind, he was forced to continue on to Malta, landing at Ta Kali after 5 hr 5 min flying time. His aircraft duly became the first Spitfire of any type to land on the island. Two weeks would pass before conditions were favourable enough for Corbishley to try to return to Benson. On 2 February he took off from Malta in an attempt to complete the task, but his aircraft was hit by flak near Leghorn and Corbishley was forced to bail out north of Pisa.

As well as routine tasks such as the coverage of ports and airfields, No 1 PRU was often given special tasks to complete. One such job was a request by the Assistant Director of Intelligence (Science), Dr Reginald Jones. At the end of January 1941, the Photographic Interpretation Unit had brought to Jones' attention a small pair of circular objects photographed by Plt Off W Panton near the village of Auderville, in the Normandy region of France. On 22 February Plt Off W K Manifould took off in N3111 (a pale green Type G) tasked with carrying out a low-level run over the site. Fifty-five minutes later, he commenced his run across the target from 300 ft. The photographs obtained showed the first clear images of a Freya radar system. The

One of the primary tasks of the PR detachment at St Eval was the monitoring of Brest, which served as the main French base for German surface vessels. On 9 January 1941, Flg Off Philip Watts of 'D' Flight No 1 PRU secured low-level obliques of the the Rade-de-Brest from 1000 ft in Spitfire I PR Type G K9787. Despite being subjected to intense flak, his excellent photographs revealed the presence of a Hipper-class heavy cruiser – the first time a German capital ship had been positively identified in the port (*Author's Collection*)

HIPPER CLASS CRUISER

BREST.—LOOKING NORTH.

aerial arrays were clearly visible, allowing technical specifications to be determined.

Four days later, the second prototype Type D (P9552) arrived at Benson. Its delivery would again allow the most distant targets to be covered following the loss of P9551.

By the spring of 1941 an increasing number of merchantmen were being sunk by U-boats. When the scale of this menace started to become apparent, No 1 PRU was tasked with covering the U-boat building yards of northern Germany. Although the unit had been visiting the German ports regularly for some months, it was only when cameras with long focal-length lenses became available that photographs of sufficient scale and quality could be obtained, enabling interpreters to begin tracking the enemy's building methods. A series of successful sorties flown over the major German ports during March 1941 allowed the scope of the U-boat building programme to be estimated for the first time with a degree of accuracy. Once it was known how many submarines were being built, and how long it took to complete a hull, it was possible to forecast the timetable for the arrival of new U-boats.

Heavily tasked with undertaking such operations, No 1 PRU gratefully received Type Fs R6902 and X4335 at Benson on 27 March. Of significance was the fact that they were the first aircraft received by the unit to be fitted with the improved Merlin 45 engine, which delivered increased performance.

The following day Plt Off G D Green carried out two runs over Brest at 22,000 ft. Forty minutes later, he was back at St Eval, where his photographs showed the presence of both *Scharnhorst* and *Gneisenau*. Such was the threat posed by the battlecruisers that the Admiralty demanded multiple sorties be flown every day to ensure their movements were tracked. For the best part of a year the major preoccupation of the St Eval-based flight would be the two vessels.

The previous month, the Joint Intelligence Committee (JIC), the body responsible for assessing all intelligence, had complained about the lack of photographs of the European hinterland. In its opinion this deficiency was due to the many conflicting demands placed upon the limited number of aircraft available. On 1 March it was decided that control of Nos 1 and 3 PRUs and the Central Interpretation Unit (CIU) would be re-centralised at the Air Ministry, rendering the new organisation operationally independent of any command in order to better employ the resources available.

April saw the endurance capabilities of the Type D utilised to the full on the 14th. The Admiralty still required that Genoa and La Spezia be covered, and it fell to 'C' Flight's Sgt W Morgan, who, after crossing a cloud-covered France, successfully photographed his objectives. Setting course for home, he again flew blind across France, aware he was facing a strong headwind. With only about five gallons of fuel remaining, Morgan began to climb in preparation for bailing out, his position unknown. As he started to gain altitude, the cloud cover broke and he could see the white cliffs of Dover. With his engine spluttering, Morgan put down in a pole-studded field near the airfield at Hawkinge. His epic flight had taken 7 hr 10 min – by far the longest Spitfire sortie to date.

On 21 April No 3 PRU's Plt Off B J McMaster made for Cologne, his aircraft, Type C X4493, carrying an F8 camera fitted with a new 40-inch lens that was making its operational debut. Unable to see his assigned target due to cloud, he photographed Rotterdam on his return.

For the month as a whole, April had been the busiest of the war to date, with No 1 PRU flying a total of 208 Spitfire sorties and No 3 PRU making a further 48. During May, the flights based at Benson continued to monitor potential invasion activity along the Channel coast and U-boat construction in the German ports, while steadily pushing deeper and deeper into enemy territory to cover new targets.

On 4 May Flt Lt Taylor encountered Bf 109s north of the Cotentin Peninsula. After covering Cherbourg from 3500 ft, he had just broken out of the top of a layer of cloud when he was immediately passed by two Bf 109s that were less than 150 ft away. Miraculously, the enemy aircraft failed to spot the Spitfire, and Taylor dropped back into the undercast and returned to base. The lack of reaction by the Germans was credited to a new off-white/pale pink camouflage scheme being tried operationally for the first time on Taylor's aircraft, Type G R7059.

Disaster struck six days later with the loss of No 1 PRU's only Type D Spitfire. Tasked with covering Stettin and Swinemünde, Sgt P A Mills took off from Mount Farm in P9552 at 1010 hrs and was never heard from again. Although the number of Type Fs on strength was slowly increasing, there was no immediate prospect of production Type Ds being available, despite their urgent need.

On 20 May Naval Intelligence received a report of capital ships leaving the Baltic. The following day, priority tasking was issued to 'D' Flight at Wick to search for signs of the naval force, with Plt Off M F Suckling (X4496) searching between Bergen and Stavanger and Flg Off C A S Greenhill (P9310) between Oslo and Kristiansand. After five hours in the air, Greenhill landed back at Wick, having photographed Oslo and Kristiansand, but he had failed to find the vessels. Unbeknown to Greenhill, Suckling had already located the ships. After crossing the Norwegian coast, he photographed one large cruiser in Hjeltefjord. He then covered Bergen, after which he observed more shipping to the southwest in Grimstadfjord, including another heavy cruiser. Subsequent analysis of his photographs

Spitfire V PR Type D R7056 was delivered to No 1 PRU on 28 August 1941. One of the initial batch of production Type Ds, it was assigned to 'D' Flight, where it was first flown operationally on 2 October when Flg Off Eric Durston was tasked with covering Lehrte and Döhren. He had to abort the sortie over the Netherlands, however, due to an oil leak and the port wing tank not feeding. Durston did manage to photograph Dordrecht, Rotterdam and The Hague as he flew home (*Spitfire AA810 on behalf of the Gunn family*)

showed that the second cruiser was actually the battleship *Bismarck* and the first was the heavy cruiser *Prinz Eugen*.

On 4 June Flg Off E G Hughes successfully covered Brest. His photographs showed that *Scharnhorst* and *Gneisenau* were still present, but the images also revealed the arrival of *Prinz Eugen*.

Three days later, the decision was made that Nos 1 and 3 PRUs would formally amalgamate. As had been previously decided, control of all PR assets would be centralised, with Benson being the main base for the new organisation. June had been particularly successful for No 1 PRU, with great progress made in the monitoring of movements of the major naval units of the Kriegsmarine. Indeed, practically every vessel larger than a destroyer had been photographed at least once. Likewise, No 3 PRU had also been very busy with 51 sorties flown without loss.

On 8 July Benson finally received the first production Type D Spitfire, R7035. It differed from the prototypes in a number of ways. Fitted with a Merlin 45, the aircraft had had the 29-gallon fuel tank in the rear fuselage removed and the capacity of the leading edge tank in each wing increased to 66 gallons for a total fuel load of 217 gallons. Although this represented a slight decrease in the total capacity, the safe operating range remained at approximately 1500 miles. The oil capacity was increased from 14 to 18 gallons, but the tank remained housed in the port mainplane. Initially, the camera fit comprised two fully interchangeable configurations. The 'W' type installation consisted of a split pair of F8 cameras mounted in the rear fuselage, while the 'X' type installation was made up of a split pair of F24 cameras and a single port-facing F24 oblique. The first 12 production Type Ds were based on the Mk I airframe, but all subsequent examples built were Mk V airframes.

On the 18th RAF Bomber Command finally informed No 3 PRU that it was to prepare to move to Benson, where it would be amalgamated with No 1 PRU. No 3 PRU's first operational sortie from its new base was carried out on 22 July when Flt Lt J H M Chisholm (X4385) obtained photographs of Saint-Pierre-Église.

That same day, images obtained by No 1 PRU of Brest revealed that *Scharnhorst* had sailed. Photographs taken 24 hours earlier by Flg Off P I Cunliffe-Lister had shown *Scharnhorst*, *Gneisenau* and *Prinz Eugen* present in their usual positions, although *Scharnhorst* was emitting smoke and some of its camouflage netting had been removed. However, it would not be long before the battlecruiser was found. On the 23rd, Flg Off Greenhill successfully covered La Pallice, and his photographs revealed a camouflaged *Scharnhorst* lying inside the pierhead of the outer jetty. Three days later, Cunliffe-Lister brought back images of Brest that showed *Scharnhorst* had returned.

On 21 July 1941 'C' Flight No 1 PRU flew six sorties from St Eval, the last of which caused quite a flap. Flg Off Philip Cunliffe-Lister's photographs of Brest showed *Scharnhorst*, *Gneisenau* and *Prinz Eugen* present in their usual positions, but the former was clearly emitting black smoke, indicating it was preparing to sail. Photographs of the port obtained the following day confirmed that *Scharnhorst* had indeed departed, along with four destroyers, and that the battlecruiser's place alongside the Torpedo Boat Station had been occupied by a 560 ft tanker (*Michael Cunliffe-Lister Collection*)

# AMALGAMATION

On 15 August Nos 1 and 3 PRUs were officially amalgamated. The latter unit initially retained its identity as a specialist bomb D/A flight, but over time it began performing the full range of tasks as carried out by No 1 PRU's other flights.

Eleven days later, AA781, which was the first production Type D Spitfire based on the Mk V airframe, was delivered to Benson. The main difference between this variant and earlier PR Spitfires was the inclusion of a purpose-built cockpit heating system.

After many months of machinations, all British-based PR assets were officially placed under a unified command structure in August 1941, thus ending unnecessary duplication of effort and improving operational efficiency. This change in organisation also corresponded with a number of important technical developments. Type D Spitfires, now flowing off the production line in sufficient quantity to replace losses and to upgrade the existing inventory, were regularly flying on operations. In addition, August also saw the first operational use of the F8 camera fitted with a 250-exposure magazine, allowing for more objectives to be covered per sortie.

In accordance with the policy of centralising control of all PR assets, the start of September saw the arrival at Benson of No 1416 (Reconnaissance) Flight. This unit had been formed on 10 March 1941 to fulfil the demands of General Officer Commanding-in-Chief Home Forces in the event of a German invasion. Based at Hendon, in northwest London, as part of RAF Army Co-operation Command, it was initially equipped with six Spitfire Type Gs. During August it was agreed that No 1416 Flight might take over certain Army demands currently being fulfilled by No 1 PRU.

The flight's first operational sortie of the war was carried out on 14 September by Flt Lt G F H Webb (X4907), who obtained oblique photographs of the coast at Saint-Vaast-la-Hougue from 3000 ft. On the 17th the flight was re-designated No 140 Sqn, but its establishment remained the same. Seven days earlier, R7039, flown by No 1 PRU's Plt Off G N Busbridge, went missing on a sortie to the Franco-Spanish frontier. It was the first operational loss of a production Type D.

On 22 September, Sqn Ldr N H E Messervy was despatched to Malta in Type D R7042 in order to photograph the bases of the *Regia Marina*. In six weeks he flew ten sorties, covering many ports on the Italian mainland and along the coast of North Africa. His imagery revealed much information on the disposition of Italian shipping. During September excellent

During September 1941 the policy of centralising control of all British-based PR assets saw the arrival at Benson of No 1416 Flight, which had been formed to fulfil demands for the British Army in the event of a German invasion. Soon re-designated No 140 Sqn, the unit was equipped with the Spitfire I PR Type G. With the threat of invasion receding, it began operating over the Continent, relieving No 1 PRU of the requirement to map enemy coastal defences for the British Army. Most of this work was initially carried out at low-level, the Type G being ideally suited to the task (*Author's Collection*)

coverage of the German shipbuilding yards had also been obtained, enabling the interpreters to identify 211 U-boats under construction. The results had not been achieved without cost, as four Spitfires and their pilots were lost on operations. For the remainder of 1941 most missions were generally routine in nature.

During December the designation system for aircraft was changed by introducing a role prefix to the mark. In the case of Spitfire reconnaissance variants, the type letter was changed to a Roman numeral, with the Type D becoming the PR IV, the Type F the PR VI and the Type G the PR VII, although it would be many months before the system was widely adopted by No 1 PRU.

On 5 December Flt Lt A E Hill obtained oblique photographs of the Cap-d'Antifer area from 200 ft. His images showed a parabolic aerial approximately ten feet in diameter on the edge of the cliffs at Bruneval. Such was the desire to find out the technical specifications of what was later identified as a Würzburg radar that a Combined Operations mission, codenamed Operation *Biting*, was planned to raid the site and take key components back to Britain for scientific analysis. The mission took place on the night of 27–28 February 1942 and was a complete success, in large part due to photographs taken by No 1 PRU.

Since June 1941 No 1 PRU had been operating a detachment from Gibraltar. Known as 'G' Flight, it had been formed to keep a watch on the North African territories of the Vichy French in the western Mediterranean. From January 1942 Spitfires were regularly detached from Britain. On the 9th Flg Off M C B Anderson and Plt Off A P L Barber flew two Type Ds (AA813 and AA815) down to Gibraltar, and over the next two weeks the pair completed 16 very successful sorties covering targets along the North African and Spanish coasts.

On 19 January, back at Benson, word was received that *Tirpitz* had been spotted off the Norwegian coast. 'C' Flight was immediately detailed to transfer to Wick in order to find the battleship. On the 23rd Flt Lt A F P Fane (R7035) located the vessel;

'Photographed Trondheim. Passing Aasfjord when I saw something hidden in the shadow at the far end. Could not believe my eyes or my luck. Did three runs over it and the next fjord and then turned for home.'

The photographs Fane obtained from 20,000 ft showed *Tirpitz* lying close inshore on the northern side of the Faettenfjord inlet. From this point forward a constant watch was maintained on the fjords around Trondheim, with daily sorties attempted from Wick. Two days later, flying from St Eval, Flg Off A H W Ball (R7055) photographed Brest. His imagery showed that *Gneisenau* had vacated the dry dock and was now alongside the quay at the Torpedo Boat Station. On 11 February the last sortie of the day to Brest showed *Prinz Eugen* and the battlecruisers present behind torpedo booms. This proved to be the last time No 1 PRU photographed the vessels in the port. That night, they steamed up the Channel in Operation *Cerberus*, passing through the Dover Strait in daylight the following morning.

Since the battlecruisers had first arrived at Brest in March 1941, more then 700 sorties had been flown over the port by No 1 PRU – six sorties per day were routinely attempted. Such extensive coverage had cost the unit nine Spitfires and their pilots.

The start of 1942 saw a technical development that would have a lasting impact on the RAF's bombing campaign with the introduction of the F52 camera. Basically an upgraded F24, the F52 was capable of using long focal-length lenses. The size of the camera when fitted with a 36-inch lens meant that it could not be carried by existing installations in the Spitfire. This led to the development of the 'Y' type installation, which consisted of a single F52 camera mounted vertically in the rear fuselage. Unlike the previous camera configurations, the 'Y' type was not interchangeable, and a number of PR IVs were permanently modified to this standard. The large-scale images produced by this configuration were ideal for D/A, and as more PR IVs were modified to carry the F52, an increasing number of sorties were flown to fulfil demands for RAF Bomber Command.

Another important development during early 1942 was the installation of a very high frequency (VHF) radio in the Spitfire PR IV. By the spring VHF radios were in widespread use, and would be fitted as standard in all new PR Spitfires.

On 3 May Flt Lt D W Steventon set out on a D/A sortie to Kiel, the port having been attacked on the night of 28–29 April. His aircraft, PR IV AB301, carried a F52 camera fitted with a 500-exposure magazine – the first time a device with this capacity had been used operationally. In a sortie lasting 4 hr 25 min, he made multiple runs over Kiel, obtaining many excellent large-scale images.

The summer of 1942 saw a new protagonist enter the bombing campaign in the form of the USAAF's Eighth Air Force. It was planned that the Americans would have their own dedicated PR assets, but whilst they built up their strength, USAAF units would have to rely on No 1 PRU for photography. Operations by American-flown PR Spitfires are detailed in Chapter Three.

## EXPANSION

When home-based PR assets were centralised at Benson during 1941, the resultant reorganisation led to an increase in No 1 PRU's establishment and, for the first time, pilots started to be allocated to the unit directly from Flying Training Command. To cope with the increased training

Type G (PR VII) X4944 of 'K' Flight No 1 PRU at Detling was one of a number of old Type Gs and Cs used in a training role. 'K' Flight was formed at the end of October 1941 to convert new pilots onto the Spitfire and prepare them for the demands of PR work. In July 1942 'K' Flight was re-designated 'B' Flight No 8(C) OTU when the training commitment was removed from No 1 PRU (*Author's Collection*)

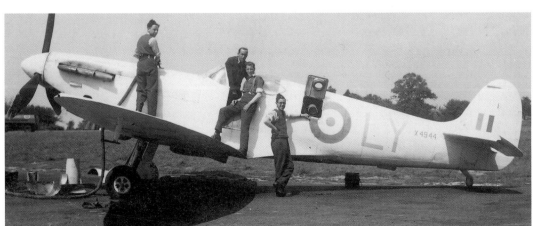

demands, 'K' Flight was formed at Benson at the end of October 1941. However, it quickly became apparent that pilots straight out of training lacked the necessary navigational skills of their predecessors.

To rectify this, the PRU Conversion Flight was formed in early January 1942 at No 3 School of General Reconnaissance. Its short course was designed to convert pilots onto Spitfires and to further their navigational skills prior to them being posted to 'K' Flight for more advanced training. In April 1942 it was decided that No 1 PRU should be absolved of its training responsibility, and this resulted in the formation of No 8 (Coastal) Operational Training Unit (No 8(C) OTU) at Fraserburgh, in Aberdeenshire, on 18 May. Four days later, the PRU Conversion Flight became 'A' Flight No 8(C) OTU, and in July 'K' Flight No 1 PRU became 'B' Flight No 8(C) OTU. During February 1943 No 8(C) OTU moved 40 miles south to Dyce, where it would remain for much of the war. Shortly after the move the unit was issued with a new establishment of 40 Spitfires (30 PR III/VI/VIIs and ten PR IVs) to reflect its increased training commitment.

Whilst No 1 PRU expanded and attempted to cover ever more targets across Europe, No 140 Sqn continued to fly sorties for the Army, its objectives generally limited to the coastal belt of France. By the start of 1942 the squadron's old Spitfire I PR Type Gs had been replaced with Spitfire V PR Type Gs (PR VIIs), as well as a number of the Spitfire V PR Type Fs (PR VIs) for longer range operations. Up until this time the majority of sorties carried out by No 140 Sqn were flown at low level, but in March an increasing number started to be undertaken at higher altitudes. On 22 June the unit received its first Spitfire PR IV, which made its operational debut on 13 July when Plt Off W J Dooley successfully photographed the area east of Paris in AB122.

During the summer No 140 Sqn was heavily involved in the preparations for the planned attack on Dieppe, codenamed Operation *Jubilee*, scheduled for 19 August. Thirteen sorties to the port were carried out during August, the last two conducted on the 17th by Plt Offs R L Jones (AR258) and L G Smith (R7116). Despite the considerable intelligence efforts made, *Jubilee* was an abject failure because much of the information gathered before the attack – most of it from aerial reconnaissance – failed to identify the strength of the defences. August had been the busiest month of the war to date for No 140 Sqn, which had undertaken nearly 200 operational sorties.

No 1 PRU's 'C' Flight, meanwhile, had been attempting to mount daily visits to Trondheim since it had discovered *Tirpitz* there on 23 January. At the end of March the flight detected the arrival of *Admiral Hipper*. Both vessels remained at Trondheim until mid-June, when they moved further north to escape the attentions of No 1 PRU's Spitfires.    (*text continues on page 44*)

Members of 'E' Flight No 1 PRU pose in front of one of their Spitfire PR IVs at Wick in August 1942. 'E' Flight had taken over coverage of Norway from 'B' Flight the previous month, by which time many of the German capital ships had moved from their anchorages at Trondheim further north up the coast beyond the range of British-based PR Spitfires. On 17 July Flt Sgt John Mair photographed *Lützow* in Lofjord and the light cruiser *Köln* in Faettenfjord in PR IV AA784. These vessels remained at Trondheim until early August, when *Köln* moved to Narvik and *Lützow* returned to Germany (*Author's Collection*)

## COLOUR PLATES

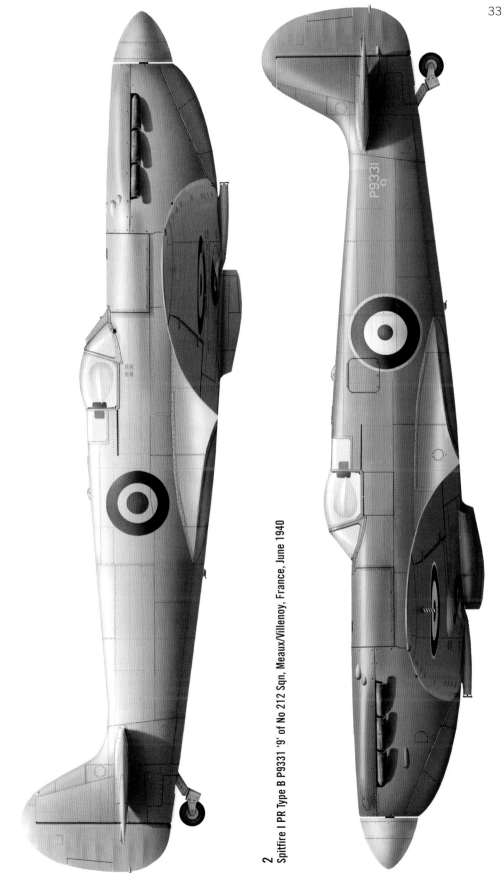

**1**
Spitfire I PR Type A N3071 of the Special Survey Flight, Nancy, France, December 1939

**2**
Spitfire I PR Type B P9331 '9' of No 212 Sqn, Meaux/Villenoy, France, June 1940

3
Spitfire I PR Type C P9550 'LY 19' of 'A' Flight PDU, Wick, Scotland, early July 1940

4
Spitfire I PR Type D P9551 'LY' of 'A' Flight No 1 PRU, Ta Kali, Malta, January 1941

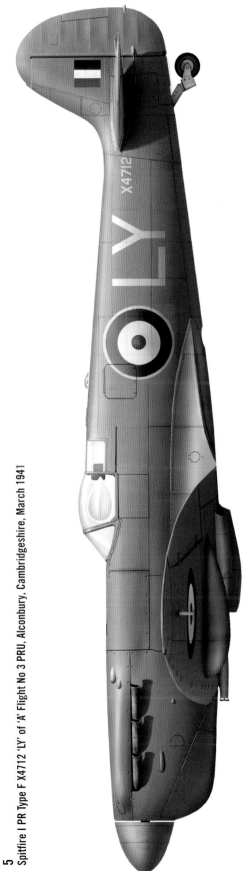

**5**
Spitfire I PR Type F X4712 'LY' of 'A' Flight No 3 PRU, Alconbury, Cambridgeshire, March 1941

**6**
Spitfire I PR Type G (serial unknown) 'ZW-J' of No 140 Sqn, Benson, South Oxfordshire, September 1941

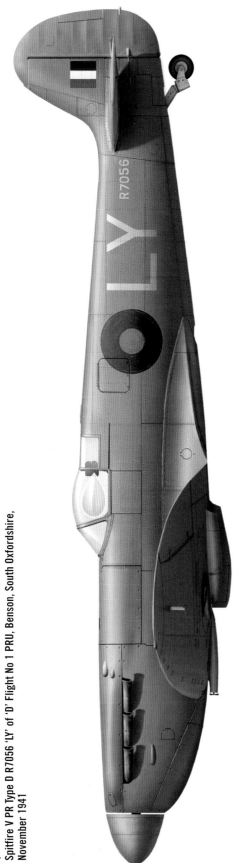

**7**
**Spitfire V PR Type D R7056 'LY' of 'D' Flight No 1 PRU, Benson, South Oxfordshire, November 1941**

**8**
**Spitfire I PR Type G (PR VII) X4944 'LY' of 'K' Flight No 1 PRU, Detling, Kent, May 1942**

**9**
Spitfire PR IV Trop AB312 of 'A' Flight No 2 PRU, LG 28/Burgh-el-Arab, Egypt, July 1942

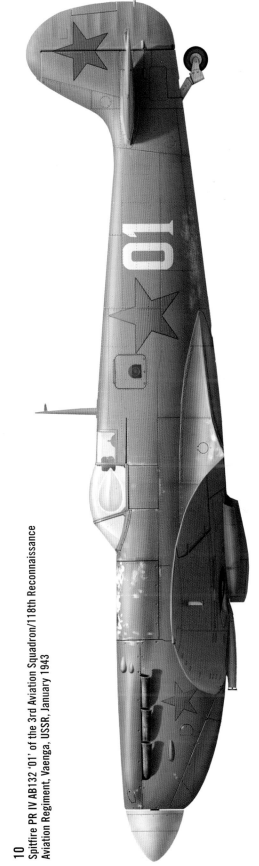

**10**
Spitfire PR IV AB132 '01' of the 3rd Aviation Squadron/118th Reconnaissance Aviation Regiment, Vaenga, USSR, January 1943

38

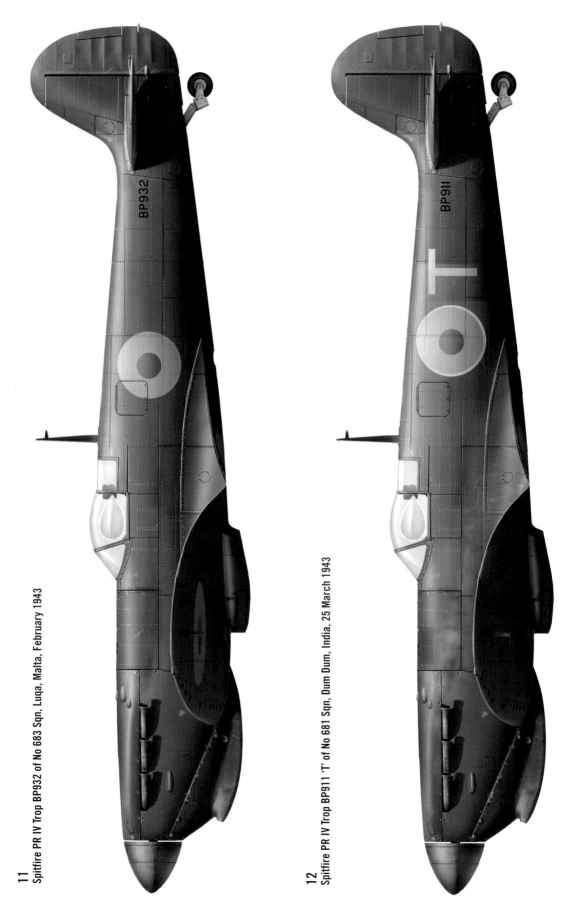

11
Spitfire PR IV Trop BP932 of No 683 Sqn, Luqa, Malta, February 1943

12
Spitfire PR IV Trop BP911 'T' of No 681 Sqn, Dum Dum, India, 25 March 1943

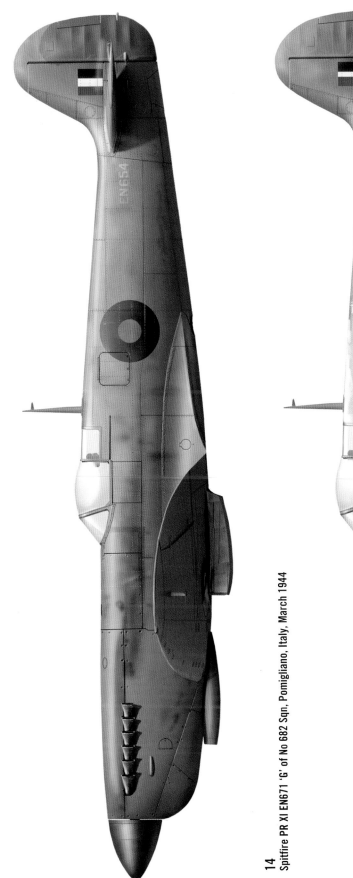
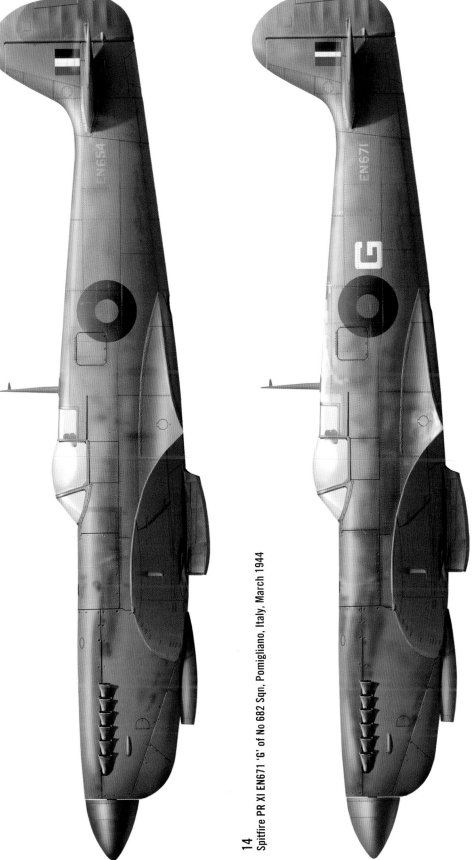

13
Spitfire PR XI EN654 of No 16 Sqn, Hartford Bridge, Hampshire, December 1943

14
Spitfire PR XI EN671 'G' of No 682 Sqn, Pomigliano, Italy, March 1944

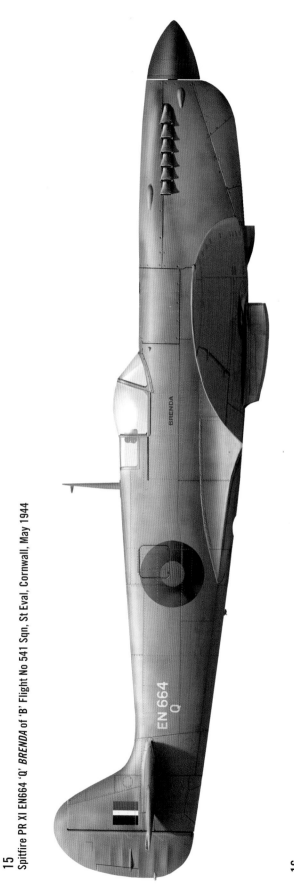

**15**
Spitfire PR XI EN664 'Q' *BRENDA* of 'B' Flight No 541 Sqn, St Eval, Cornwall, May 1944

**16**
Spitfire PR X MD193 of No 541 Sqn, Benson, South Oxfordshire, 4 June 1944

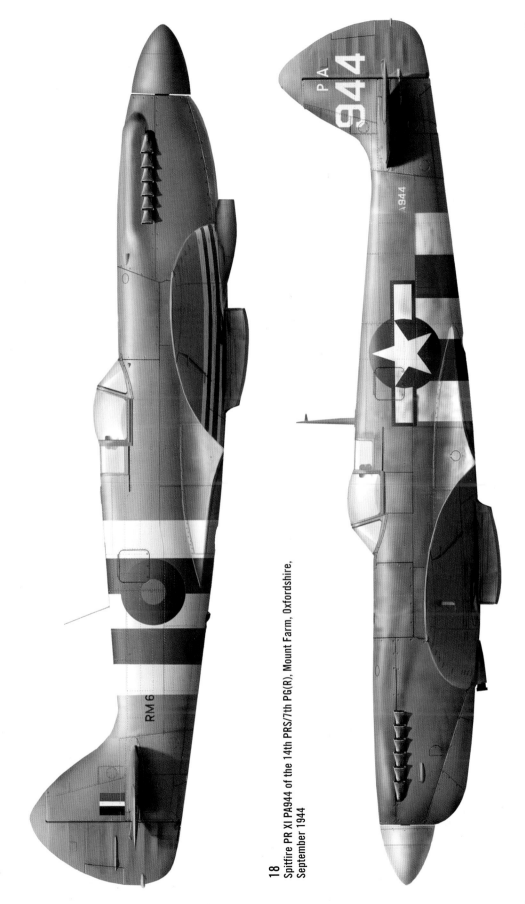

**17**
Spitfire PR XIX RM633 of No 541 Sqn, Benson, South Oxfordshire, June 1944

**18**
Spitfire PR XI PA944 of the 14th PRS/7th PG(R), Mount Farm, Oxfordshire, September 1944

42

**19**
Spitfire PR XI PL969 'P' of the Forward Detachment No 681 Sqn, Monywa, Burma, February 1945

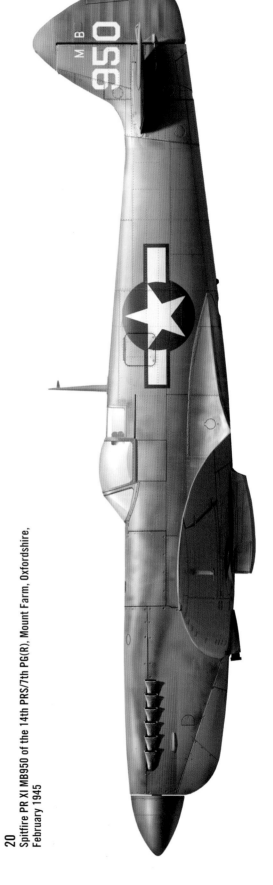

**20**
Spitfire PR XI MB950 of the 14th PRS/7th PG(R), Mount Farm, Oxfordshire, February 1945

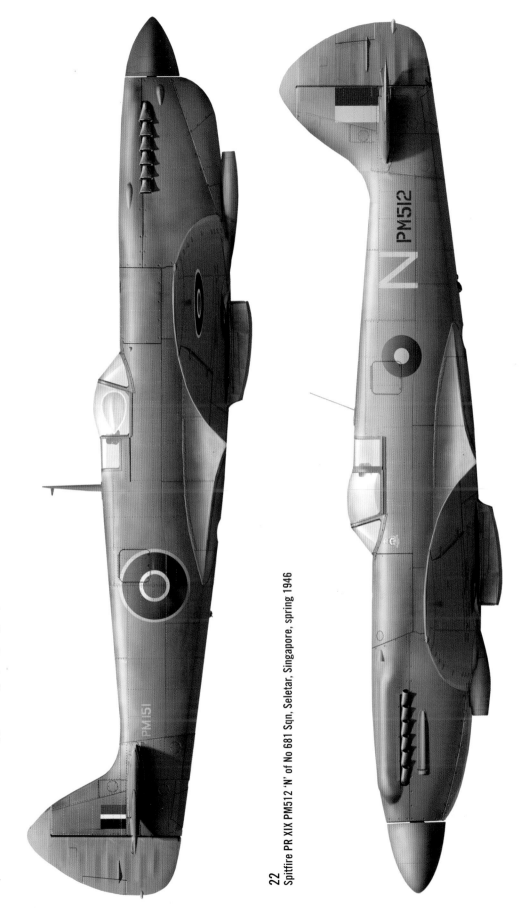

21
Spitfire PR XI PM151 of No 400 Sqn, Petit Brogel (B90), Belgium, March 1945

22
Spitfire PR XIX PM512 'N' of No 681 Sqn, Seletar, Singapore, spring 1946

The presence of major naval units in northern Norway posed a significant threat to Allied shipping headed to the Soviet Union. With convoy PQ 18 set to sail for Archangelsk on 2 September 1942, it was decided to send a strike force of Hampden torpedo-bombers to operate from Murmansk. Under the codename Operation *Orator*, the Hampdens would be supported by a small detachment of No 1 PRU Spitfires that would provide reconnaissance over the northern fjords of Norway, which were beyond the range of British-based aircraft. On 1 September three Spitfire PR IVs flown by Flt Lt E A Fairhurst, Flg Off D R M Furniss and Plt Off G W Walker set off for Vaenga, near Murmansk, where they would be based for the duration of *Orator*. Throughout the course of the detachment the Spitfires would carry Soviet national insignia in place of their RAF markings.

On the 11th, Flt Lt Fairhurst (BP889) flew the detachment's first sortie when he covered Altafjord from 22,000 ft. His photographs showed the presence of the *Admiral Scheer*, *Admiral Hipper* and the light cruiser *Köln* in Kåfjord. The detachment returned to Britain in mid-October, having flown 15 successful sorties. Its Spitfires were handed over to the Air Force of the Northern Fleet (*Voyenno-Vozdushnye Sily Severnyy Flot* – VVS SF).

## MEDITERRANEAN OPERATIONS

Whilst home-based PR assets increased in strength and capability, overseas reconnaissance units were forced to rely on aircraft already in-theatre. It would be 1942 before the first PR Spitfires were permanently based abroad.

On 7 March the first Spitfire PR IV (AB300) arrived on Malta, where it was pressed into service with No 69 Sqn. The embattled island's position in the middle of the Mediterranean meant it was perfectly placed to monitor shipping carrying supplies to Axis forces in North Africa. AB300 carried out its first operational sortie from Malta on the 12th, when Plt Off P J Kelley successfully covered targets in Sicily. As more PR IVs gradually arrived they were formed into their own flight, and for long periods of time the PR Spitfires were the only aircraft capable of operating from Malta in daylight due to persistent Axis attacks.

PR IV AB312 was one of the first PR Spitfires to be delivered to 'A' Flight No 2 PRU in the Western Desert in March 1942. Seen here during the summer of that same year, it was lost on 16 October when Flg Off John Bird failed to return from a sortie to cover Bardia, Sollum and Mersa Matruh on the Libya–Egypt border. The pilot had probably fallen victim to the severe weather conditions reported over the whole area by other aircraft (*Author's Collection*)

On 12 August three more PR IVs were delivered to No 69 Sqn's Spitfire Flight, now known as 'B' Flight, to augment operations. Three days later, five merchantmen from the Operation *Pedestal* convoy reached Malta, bringing enough supplies to allow more anti-shipping operations to be carried out. This in turn meant that the Spitfires of 'B' Flight were tasked with monitoring the arrival and departure of Axis vessels from Benghazi and the main Italian ports.

At the eastern end of the Mediterranean, the threat posed by the Italians in North Africa and the Dodecanese led to the formation of No 2 PRU at Heliopolis, in Egypt. Initially equipped with Hurricanes, it would be 1942 before any Spitfires were on strength. The first PR IVs were received in March, with the unit's operational diary for the 17th noting that three Spitfire V PR Type Ds had arrived from Britain. Over the next few days the aircraft were tested and camouflaged in No 2 PRU's Royal Blue. This dark blue scheme had been used by the unit since 1941, when it was found to better blend in with the clearer conditions normally found at altitude in the Middle East.

On 29 March Flt Lt S N Pearce flew BP883 on the unit's first operational Spitfire sortie when he successfully covered Patras, in Greece. On 7 May Spitfires BP882 and BP883 were flown to Gambut, in Libya, where they became a permanently detached desert flight. Henceforth known as 'A' Flight, they were tasked with carrying out reconnaissance for the Eighth Army. On 7 August 'A' Flight joined No 285 (Reconnaissance) Wing, which had been formed to coordinate all operations by tactical and strategic reconnaissance assets in the Western Desert. While 'A' Flight flew missions in direct support of the Army, 'B' Flight at Heliopolis continued with photographing strategic targets. Much of its attention at this time was focused on Tobruk, in Libya, and Crete.

By October the British Army had built up its strength and was ready to launch a new offensive at El Alamein. During the month 'A' Flight was heavily engaged in preparations for the forthcoming attack, with every yard of the proposed battlefield being covered by large-scale photographs. On 23 October the Eighth Army began its assault, and by 4 November Axis forces had begun to retreat westward. As the Eighth Army advanced through Cyrenaica, 'A' Flight was hot on its heels, moving five times during the month before ending up at Timimi, in Libya, on the 20th. After a pause in the fighting, the Eighth Army resumed its advance with an attack on Generalfeldmarschall Rommel's position at Buerat, in Libya, on 15 January 1943.

Six days later, Plt Off D W Barbour covered targets in Tunisia – the first time any objectives in the country had been photographed by No 2 PRU. On the 26th the flight moved again, this time to Castel Benito, in Libya, from where work began on obtaining large-scale photographic coverage of the new enemy positions at Mareth, in Tunisia. In line with the Air Ministry's policy of restructuring the PR organisation in the Mediterranean, No 2 PRU became No 680 Sqn at the end of the month.

## OPERATION *TORCH*

On 8 November 1942, Anglo-American forces commenced Operation *Torch* when they invaded Vichy French North Africa with landings in

Morocco and Algeria. During this period the Spitfires of No 69 Sqn's 'B' Flight were heavily involved in tracking the movements of the *Regia Marina* in case it attempted to interfere with Allied invasion shipping. By the 10th the Vichy French in North Africa had capitulated, allowing the Allies to begin advancing on Tunisia.

It had been recognised in the planning for *Torch* that there would be the need for an organic PRU in-theatre. For the British, Eastern Air Command was formed to control RAF resources, and it was to this command that a new reconnaissance unit was allocated. No 4 PRU had been formed at Benson on 10 September 1942 with an establishment of six Spitfire PR IVs.

On 13 November No 4 PRU transferred to Maison Blanche, in Algeria. The first operational sortie flown by the unit in North Africa was carried out on the 17th by Flg Off D M McKenzie (BR423), when he successfully covered Bizerte and Tunis. On the evening of the 20th, however, Maison Blanche was attacked by Luftwaffe bombers. Three of No 4 PRU's Spitfires were destroyed and two damaged. The next operational sortie was not flown until the 24th, when Sgt B J O'Connell successfully covered Gabès and Tunis in the unit's sole remaining Spitfire, BR664.

Replacement aircraft from Britain enabled No 4 PRU to pick up the pace of operations during December, with 42 sorties flown, of which 28 obtained photographs. The cost had been high, however, with four pilots lost. The superior performance of the Bf 109Gs and Fw 190s in Tunisia often made operations prohibitive, which led Eastern Air Command to petition the Air Ministry for No 4 PRU to be re-equipped with Spitfire PR XIs.

The winter of 1942–43 also saw No 69 Sqn's 'B' Flight carry out numerous sorties, the majority of which were to Sicily and southern Italy. However, targets in Tunisia, Libya, Greece and Sardinia were also covered, the latter due to No 4 PRU's paucity of aircraft. By the start of February 1943, the only Axis forces that remained in North Africa were in Tunisia. The shrinking of the enemy perimeter led to PRUs from three different RAF commands operating over the same area with little coordination. The decision was duly made to reorganise PR in the Mediterranean, as detailed in Chapter 5.

In the lead up to Operation *Torch*, it was not just Vichy French holdings in North Africa that attracted the attention of the RAF. Their territories in West Africa also featured in the lenses of PR Spitfires. On 27 October 1942, PR IVs BR642 and BR667 were allocated to No 128 Sqn to carry out long-range missions to Senegal to monitor a number of major Vichy French naval vessels located there. In early November the Spitfires flew to Yundum, at Bathurst in Gambia, where the squadron was already operating a detachment. Over the course of the next few weeks both aircraft flew numerous sorties to Senegal and obtained coverage of the capital, Dakar, and all of the principal airfields in the country.

Following the *Torch* landings, the Vichy French in West Africa joined the Allies and by December the small West African PRU had received orders to cease operations. Although No 128 Sqn had only operated Spitfires for a short period, their superior performance had enabled the unit to fulfil the photographic demands made of it.

# CHAPTER THREE

# STRATEGIC RECCE IN NORTHWEST EUROPE

In an effort to improve performance, the Spitfire PR IX was introduced as a stopgap measure until the purpose-built PR XI became available. Converted from a standard Spitfire F IX, the first PR IX arrived at Benson in October 1942. On 7 February 1943, this aircraft, PR IX EN149, flown by No 541 Sqn's Flg Off Alex Glover, made the first attempt to cover the Möhne Dam as part of the preparations for Operation *Chastise*, the planned attack on the Ruhr dams. EN149 was later converted to PR XI standard (as seen here) and served with No 4 Sqn (*Peter Arnold Collection*)

By 1942 No 1 PRU had grown into a huge organisation, with nine operational flights covering a vast geographical area. In August the Air Ministry authorised the unit to be split into five new squadrons. On 19 October a PR wing was formed at Benson comprising No 540 Sqn with two flights of Mosquitos, Nos 541, 542 and 543 Sqns each with two flights of Spitfires, and No 544 Sqn, which included the Spitfires formerly of 'G' Flight No 1 PRU, which became 'B' Flight and continued to operate from Gibraltar. The three Spitfire squadrons were each established for 20 aircraft, comprising 16 PR IVs and four PR VIIs, whilst 'B' Flight No 544 Sqn was allocated three PR IVs.

By mid-1942 the Spitfire PR IV was outclassed by the latest German fighters, with losses steadily climbing, particularly on operations over northwest Germany. A request was made for standard Spitfire F IXs to be converted for the PR role until the purpose-built PR XI became available.

During October, Spitfire BS473 – the first of 16 PR IXs – was delivered to Benson. The variant retained the Merlin 61 engine of the F IX, and was configured for either a 'W' or 'Y' type camera installation. Although the armoured windscreen and weapons were removed, the PR IX was not fitted with the 'wet' wing of the PR IV and only had an 85-gallon internal fuel capacity that could be supplemented with a single under-fuselage slipper tank. All machines were camouflaged PRU Blue and most served briefly with Nos 541 and 542 Sqns.

At the start of December No 541 Sqn took delivery of its first PR XI, BS499. Originally intended to be based on the Spitfire VIII airframe, delays in that programme led to the PR XI being based on the Spitfire IX instead. The PR XI had a top speed of 422 mph and could reach an altitude of 44,000 ft, although the lack of a pressurised cockpit limited the amount of time a pilot could operate at such heights. The PR XI retained the leading edge wing tanks of the PR IV for a total internal fuel capacity of 217 gallons, although the higher fuel consumption associated with the Merlin 61 reduced its safe range to about 1300 miles. From late 1944 onwards, the capability to carry a single slipper-type drop tank was introduced. An enlarged oil tank of 14.4-gallon capacity was fitted under the engine and enclosed by an enlarged chin fairing.

As was now standard, all PR XIs were fitted with VHF radios and unarmoured windscreens and camouflaged in PRU Blue. Some early models were fitted with teardrop canopy fairings, but most had the bulged Malcolm Hood. One feature of the Spitfire VIII to be incorporated in the PR XI was a retractable tail wheel, which reduced drag in flight.

The camera installations of the first PR XIs were the 'W', 'X' or 'Y' types, but soon the universal or 'U' type installation was developed that allowed for a vertical split pair of F52 cameras each with a 36-inch lens to be fitted in the rear fuselage. Another modification was the addition of mud flaps and oil traps on the ventral camera ports to stop lens fouling. For PR XIs employed in a tactical role, provision was made for the installation of a F24 camera in each wing. For low-level vertical photography, each camera was fitted with a five-inch lens, and in the case of oblique photography, the cameras were configured to face forward and were fitted with eight-inch lenses. Another special fit for low-level work utilised two moving film strip F52 cameras fitted with 36-inch lenses. Subsequently known as the F63, the moving film compensated for aircraft movement during exposure to reduce image blurring at low altitude.

A second PR XI, BS498, was received by No 541 Sqn on 4 December, and it was this machine that attempted the first operational sortie by the type on the 10th when Flt Lt Fairhurst was tasked with covering targets in Holland and the Ruhr. By early 1943 PR IV production had ceased, a total of 229 having been built, but it would be some time before the PR XI was available in significant numbers.

The first operational PR XI loss occurred on 7 February 1943 when No 541 Sqn's Flg Off J C Taffs (EN385) went missing on a sortie to the Ruhr. By this time the squadron was responsible for covering targets in the zone known as the 'Southern Area', which encompassed France, Belgium and southern Germany, whilst No 542 Sqn covered the 'Northern Area' comprising the Netherlands, northern Germany and Denmark. 'B' Flight No 543 Sqn was also covering targets in the 'Southern Area', but it was increasingly being used as an unofficial OTU. At St Eval, No 543 Sqn's 'A' Flight was responsible for covering western

When No 1 PRU was split into squadrons in October 1942, Wg Cdr Spencer Ring became Wing Commander Operations at Benson. He successfully argued for the retention of Spitfire PR XI production when it appeared it would be phased out in favour of the Mosquito (*Author's Collection*)

France down to the Spanish border. By March, Nos 541 and 542 Sqns were operating exclusively from Benson due to the arrival of the USAAF's 13th Photographic Squadron (PS) at Mount Farm on 16 February 1943.

Just as the abilities of the PR XI were starting to be proven over Europe, the future of the type was put in question. At the end of 1942 it was proposed that all PRUs should convert to the Mosquito because of ongoing production delays with the PR XI. Wing Commander Operations at Benson, Wg Cdr Ring, pointed out that the Spitfire PR XI was much more capable of evading intercepting fighters than the Mosquito, and for short and medium range work it was far more economical. Furthermore, the PR XI enjoyed considerably higher serviceability rates than the Mosquito.

At a meeting at the Air Ministry in March 1943 it was argued that Spitfires should be retained, and that the PR organisation would be better served with half of the squadrons being equipped with the latest PR XIs and the remainder operating the Mosquito for longer-ranged work. It was concluded that production of the PR XI would not be phased out and would actually be increased and accelerated. The PR XI duly remained in production until late 1944, by which point it had become the most numerous version of all PR Spitfires with 471 built, including 14 converted PR IXs.

Whilst the future of the Spitfire PR XI was in the balance, another variant was being developed for low-level work. Known as the PR XIII, it was basically a PR VII fitted with a Merlin 32 engine that was specially rated for low-altitude operations. The prototypes were tested at the end of 1942, and a total of 26 examples were converted from existing Spitfire F Vs and PR VIIs. The PR XIII retained the 'G' type camera installation, but the 29-gallon fuel tank in the fuselage was deleted, leaving an internal fuel load of only 85 gallons, which was supplemented by a slipper tank. Armament was partially retained, with those aircraft converted from 'A' wing machines keeping eight 0.303-inch machines guns and those from 'B' wing fighters retaining just four 0.303-inch guns after their twin 20 mm cannon were removed.

The first two examples, W3135 and BM447 (both four-gun aircraft), were delivered to Benson on 5 April 1943. By this time the use of dedicated aircraft for 'dicing' was already waning, with the preference being to use standard PR aircraft fitted with oblique cameras. PR XIIIs remained in use at Benson with Nos 541 and No 542 Sqns until 1944, but saw little operational flying.

In an effort to cripple the German war effort, RAF Bomber Command was constantly looking for vulnerable industries to target in order to create production bottlenecks. The Ruhr was a major industrial area that was home to factories involved in vital war production. A key source of power for this area was derived from the Möhne, Sorpe and Eder dams, and any successful attack on these targets would seriously impact production.

On 25 January 1943, a request was made to Benson for coverage of the Möhnesee and its dam. The first attempt was carried out on 7 February by No 541 Sqn's Flg Off A Glover (PR IX EN149), but on arrival in the area he found all of his objectives obscured by cloud. It was not until the 19th that large-scale photographs were obtained, following a successful mission over the dam by Flt Lt R C Cussons (PR IX EN151). A further request was received on 5 May to cover the Sorpe and Eder dams, with these being successfully photographed on the 13th by Flg Off G W Puttick (PR IX BS502) of No 542 Sqn.

On the night of 16–17 May No 617 Sqn carried out Operation *Chastise*, which saw its crews attack the dams with Upkeep bouncing bombs dropped from modified Lancaster B III (Special) heavy bombers. The following morning, No 542 Sqn's Flg Off F G Fray (PR XI EN343) obtained excellent quality, large-scale photographs of the Möhne and Sorpe dams. Fray's images showed that the Möhne dam had a huge breach, but that the Sorpe dam was intact. On the 18th, Flg Off D G Scott succeeded in covering the Eder dam, his photographs showing it was physically breached, and that flooding had extended as far as Kassel. The target photographs obtained by Nos 541 and 542 Sqns prior to the attack played a major part in the success of the operation, and the D/A imagery post-raid confirmed that *Chastise* had been a great success.

Just weeks prior to the dams raid, it had been decided that a small ferry training unit would be formed within No 543 Sqn so that PR aircrew to be posted overseas would be given additional training. On 22 April this unit was officially named No 309 Ferry Training and Aircraft Despatch Unit (No 309 FT&ADU) and it was made independent of No 543 Sqn. No 309 FT&ADU was based at Benson, and for the remainder of the war all PR aircrew destined for overseas would pass through the unit.

In an effort to cripple war production in the Ruhr, the RAF planned to destroy the dams that produced much of the power on which the region depended. On 5 April 1943, No 541 Sqn's Flg Off James Brew covered the Möhnesee and its dam from 27,500 ft in PR XI BS499. It was just one of the many sorties flown to photograph the dams in preparation for RAF Bomber Command's attack on the night of 16–17 May *(Author's Collection)*

At the end of April RAF Coastal Command advocated for a reorganisation of the PR structure so that the units at Benson and Dyce, where No 8(C) OTU was now based, were brought under one unified command. On 26 June the Air Ministry authorised the formation of No 106(PR) Wing, headquartered at Benson. The new wing would control the existing reconnaissance wing, which consisted of five squadrons (Nos 540–544), No 309 FT&ADU and No 8(C) OTU. No 106(PR) Wing was officially formed on 3 July, and was responsible for the operational control and training of all of the RAF's strategic PR assets in Britain.

Aside from special operations such as supporting *Chastise*, Spitfire-equipped PR units remained firmly committed to covering the major naval units of the Kriegsmarine in 1943. The location of *Tirpitz* and other warships in northern Norway caused the Admiralty to examine how best to attack these vessels when they were beyond the range of the RAF's heavy bombers. It eventually settled on Operation *Source*, which would see the vessels at anchor attacked by specifically developed X-class midget submarines.

For *Source* to work, naval planners required exact knowledge of the location and defences of the ship being targeted – information that could only be obtained through PR. Arrangements were made to operate a small detachment of Spitfires from Vaenga, as they had done in 1942. Although the RAF had not been able to track the movements of *Tirpitz* since March, the Soviets had been endeavouring to photograph it using the Spitfire PR IVs that had been left behind at the end of *Orator*. The three aircraft had joined the 3rd Aviation Squadron of the Vaenga-based 118th Reconnaissance

Flg Off Roy Kenwright of No 543 Sqn's 'A' Flight stands on the wing root of one of the unit's PR XIs at St Eval in March 1943. No 543 Sqn was formed from No 1 PRU's 'C' and 'D' Flights in October 1942 when No 1 PRU was split into five new squadrons. 'A' Flight No 543 Sqn took over responsibility for covering the ports and airfields along France's western coast. Kenwright initially served with No 542 Sqn before joining No 543 Sqn, and he was one of the pilots who flew from Vaenga during Operation *Source*. On his second operational tour Kenwright served with No 682 Sqn in Italy (*Author's Collection*)

Aviation Regiment, which was part of the Northern Fleet. From the start of May 1943 the 3rd Aviation Squadron covered Altafjord, and from the photographs obtained the battlecruiser *Scharnhorst* and the heavy cruiser *Lützow* were identified.

On the morning of 3 September No 543 Sqn's Sqn Ldr F A Robinson (BR658) and Flg Offs J H Dixon (AB427) and B R Kenwright (AB423) took off for Vaenga, all arriving safely after a flight time of five hours. The detachment's first successful sortie was flown on the 7th by Flg Off Dixon (AB427) when he covered Langfjord. Based on the photographs obtained, six Royal Navy X-craft carried out their attack on the ships in Altafjord on 22 September, with two of them causing extensive damage to *Tirpitz*.

The day after the operation, both Kenwright and Dixon covered the fjord. Their photographs revealed that *Tirpitz* was leaking oil. The last *Source* sortie was flown on 23 October by Dixon, his photographs showing that *Tirpitz* was the only major naval unit remaining in Altafjord. The RAF detachment had flown a total of 31 sorties, of which 25 were successful. The information obtained from the photographs prior to the attack was described by the senior naval commander involved in *Source* as 'invaluable' to the success of the operation. With the end of the detachment, its Spitfires were also handed over to the Soviets.

## OPTIMUM STRENGTH

By September the establishment of aircraft in No 106(PR) Wing had reached its target level of 40 Spitfires and 40 Mosquitos, with Nos 541 and 542 Sqns both being equipped with 20 Spitfire PR XIs. As a consequence, No 543 Sqn was disbanded on 18 October. That month also saw No 544 Sqn convert solely to the Mosquito PR IX when its old 'B' Flight, which had been operating Spitfire PR IVs from Gibraltar, was absorbed by No 541 Sqn. From this point forward the four squadrons of No 106(PR) Wing, together with the USAAF PRU at Mount Farm, would fulfil the strategic reconnaissance demands of all British-based commands and agencies.

On 3 November No 541 Sqn flew six PR XI sorties to the Pas-de-Calais, all of which obtained large-scale images of their objectives. The photographs showed a number of sites with exactly the same layout of buildings and identical features, with the location at Bois-Carré being the most advanced. Each site consisted of a platform or ramp aimed in the direction of London and three ski-shaped buildings. The imagery caused consternation at the JIC, which believed the sites were related to Germany's long-range weapons programme. It duly ordered that a thorough search be carried out along the French coast for what became known as 'Bois-Carré' sites. Work in connection with the search was given the codename *Crossbow*.

By the end of the month 72 sites had been identified, and the breakthrough occurred on 28 November when large-scale photographs of Peenemünde showed a small aircraft at the base of one of the ramps. This confirmed that the locations in France were firing sites for some kind of flying bomb.

December saw intensive attacks commenced on the *Crossbow* launch sites by RAF bombers of the 2nd Tactical Air Force (TAF) and the USAAF's VIII Bomber Command under the codename *Noball*. These attacks required immediate D/A sorties to be flown, with No 542 Sqn called upon to provide photographic coverage. The Spitfires of No 106(PR) Wing were largely responsible for identifying the first long-range V1 flying bomb, and its launch sites, and then monitoring enemy efforts to bring the weapon system into service.

## USAAF PR SPITFIRES

Since March 1943 the USAAF had been carrying out strategic reconnaissance operations from Mount Farm with its 13th PS. This unit was joined by the 14th and 22nd PSs during the summer, which were formed into the newly activated 7th Photographic Reconnaissance and Mapping Group (PRMG) on 7 July 1943 – the latter had only just been transferred to England from the USA.

Although the 7th was part of the Eighth Air Force, the poor altitude performance of its F-5A Lightnings meant that many requests for photographic coverage by VIII Bomber Command had to be passed on to the RAF's No 106(PR) Wing. Delays in obtaining improved versions of the F-5 led to the Eighth Air Force requesting 12 Spitfire PR XIs for use by the 7th PRMG, the first example (MB945) being delivered on 1 November. Two days later, Maj M Wayne of the 14th PS carried out the group's first operational Spitfire sortie in the same aircraft when he attempted to cover airfields in France.

The relatively poor performance of the F-5A Lightning and delays in obtaining improved versions of the aircraft led the Eighth Air Force to request Spitfire PR XIs for its own use. MB950 was one of the first machines delivered to the 7th PG(R) during November 1943. Initially, the Spitfires were not assigned to a particular squadron, but in January 1944 the decision was made that the 14th PRS would carry out all of the group's Spitfire operations *(Author's Collection)*

During November a number of designation changes took place, with each squadron now being known as a photographic reconnaissance squadron (PRS) and the group re-designated as the 7th Photographic Group (Reconnaissance) (7th PG(R)).

The following month saw more distant objectives covered, with many sorties being flown in support of VIII Bomber Command. However, the increased rate of operations soon led to the group's first PR XI loss when, on 23 December, Capt S A Scott of the 22nd PRS failed to return from a sortie to Münster and Osnabrück in PA851.

At the start of January 1944, the decision was made that the 14th PRS would be the sole operator of the 7th PG(R)'s Spitfires. One pilot who flew PR XIs with the 14th during 1944 was Lt J S Blyth. Originally trained to fly the F-5 with the 22nd PRS, he transferred to the 14th PRS in April;

'I was impressed with the PR XI's speed, and how it handled at altitude. I had previously flown the F-5, but its performance at height was poor. In comparison, the Spitfire was very responsive above 30,000 ft and still had a good rate of climb. Because of all the problems with the F-5, the Spitfires did the longer range work. I was fortunate to fly such a great airplane [sic], and did not mind long-range missions. My only criticism of the Spitfire was that compared to the F-5, the cockpit was cramped, but it was a small price to pay. I would take my little old Spit any day – it saved my life.'

Blyth flew 38 sorties in PR XIs and covered targets as far afield as Munich, Schweinfurt and Berlin.

## PREPARING FOR *OVERLOAD*

By March 1944, as well as constant coverage of *Crossbow* sites, demands were also increasing for photographic cover of a multitude of targets related to Operation *Overlord*, the planned invasion of northern France. Much of the early work was undertaken by No 140 Sqn, but this was often supplemented by the Spitfire units at Benson.

March had also seen RAF Bomber Command carry out numerous attacks on French marshalling yards for Supreme Headquarters Allied Expeditionary Force (SHAEF), which requested that No 106(PR) Wing

Spitfire PR XI MB793 'H' was assigned to No 542 Sqn at Benson on 21 June 1943. Seen here in the early spring of 1944, the aircraft continued to serve with the unit until 7 May 1944 when it suffered an inflight engine failure and its pilot was forced to crash land. The damage was serious enough for MB793 to be struck off charge (*Author's Collection*)

carry out the D/A work. On 27 April No 542 Sqn's Flt Sgt E G Bacon (EN658) covered *Crossbows* in the Cherbourg area. When his photographs were analysed, they revealed a new site near Le Bel Hamelin. Closer examination showed that it was probably a launch site, but it did not conform to the standard pattern, with fewer buildings being visible. From then on more of these modified sites started to show up on photographs.

Even though the Spitfire PR XI still maintained a healthy high-altitude performance advantage over frontline German fighters at this stage in the conflict, the RAF realised that it would only be a matter of time before the enemy developed improved types. This led to the introduction of the first purpose-built high-altitude PR Spitfire in the form of the PR X. Based on the F VII and fitted with the pressure cabin and retractable tailwheel of the latter, it was equipped with a Merlin 64. The PR X was fitted with the 'U' type camera installation and the 'wet' wing of the PR XI.

Performance was generally similar to the PR XI, but the main difference was the inclusion of a pressurised cockpit. The small pressure differential created an environment equivalent to an altitude many thousands of feet lower, thus enabling the pilot to withstand great heights for longer periods of time. The cockpit canopy was double glazed, and for improved visibility the PR X was fitted with a bulged Malcolm Hood of the Lobelle type. In total only 16 PR Xs were built, and they all served with Nos 541 and 542 Sqns from May 1944 through to August 1945. The first example, MD193, was delivered to No 541 Sqn on 8 May, and it made the type's operational debut three days later when Flt Lt L H Scargill undertook a mission to the Pas-de-Calais area.

Invasion stripes are painted on one of No 541 Sqn's Spitfire PR Xs at Benson. On 3 June 1944, instructions were received to apply invasion markings to all of No 106(PR) Group's aircraft under the proviso that operations on the 4th be kept to a minimum with aeroplanes so marked, but that from the 5th onwards only aircraft with invasion stripes should be flown (*Author's Collection*)

May also saw the final reorganisation of British-based strategic reconnaissance assets. Although the wing headquarters set up in 1943 had functioned extremely well, the USAAF's desire to create an independent organisation to control its own reconnaissance forces in Britain prior to the invasion of Europe had created a certain amount of tension. Over the course of many meetings at the highest levels, the Eighth Air Force was eventually persuaded that its aims would be better served by maintaining a combined and integrated command.

A new Anglo-American body known as the Joint Photographic Reconnaissance Committee (JPRC) would be formed to assess and prioritise photographic demands. The JPRC would examine all requests for PR and, as a sub-committee of the JIC, would have access to the highest intelligence sources to aid in prioritising tasks. No 106(PR) Group would be formed from No 106(PR) Wing and retain all of the units under the latter's command. No 106(PR) Group and the JPRC both came into being on 15 May 1944, with the new group answering directly to the latter.

With the invasion of northern France scheduled for summer 1944, one of the most important tasks related to *Overlord* was the destruction of the enemy radar network. Since the earliest days of the PRU, locating the positions of German wireless and radar sites had been a top priority, and as such much was known about the enemy's radar installations. On 22 May 1944, fighter-bombers commenced concentrated attacks on the coastal radar sites, and two days later No 541 Sqn began obtaining high-altitude D/A photographs of each site. By D-Day transmissions were detected at only five out of 98 sites, and even these were not capable of full operation. The success of the PR organisation in identifying all of the enemy's radar installations was a major contributing factor to the initial success of the invasion.

While No 541 Sqn was committed to covering pre-invasion targets in France, No 542 Sqn continued to fly sorties to Germany and Holland. As well as the usual visits to the northern ports to monitor U-boat construction, numerous D/A sorties were flown to the likes of Brunswick and the Ruhr.

On 12 September 1943, Kapitan Leonid Ilyich Yelkin, commander of the 118th Reconnaissance Aviation Regiment's 3rd Aviation Squadron, attempted a low-level sortie in Spitfire PR IV BP891 to photograph German capital ships in Norwegian fjords. Although the images he brought back were too indistinct due to mist and rain to allow positive identification, they did confirm the presence of large vessels in Kaafjord and Langfjord. On 29 February 1944, Yelkin, who had been made a Hero of the Soviet Union on 22 January, was tasked with covering *Tirpitz* in Altafjord in a PR IV but he failed to return to Vaenga (*Author's Collection*)

May also proved to be a very busy month for the USAAF Spitfires at Mount Farm, with the 14th PRS flying 72 sorties. Much of the work was associated with Eighth Air Force raids on German oil installations, but as more heavy bombers were called upon to strike French marshalling yards and conduct *Noball* attacks, an increasing number of sorties were flown to France.

Whilst much of the PR in relation to *Overlord* was of a routine nature, there was one special operation undertaken by the Spitfires of No 106(PR) Wing in the run-up to the invasion that was vitally important. *Tirpitz* had remained in northern Norway since it was seriously damaged during Operation *Source*. At the end of 1943, the Royal Navy began to formulate plans for another attack on the vessel, and it quickly concluded that a carrier strike was the most likely to succeed. Operation *Tungsten* was scheduled to take place in March 1944, and in order to maximise the chances of success, up-to-date photographs of *Tirpitz*'s anchorage would be required. In order for these to be obtained, Spitfire PR IVs would be taken out of storage and three deployed to Vaenga.

With the return of sufficient photographic light at the end of February, the Royal Navy requested that Soviet Spitfire PR IVs of the 3rd Aviation Squadron resume operations over Altafjord. On 29 February Kapitán L I Yelkin attempted to cover the anchorage in a PR IV but failed to return to Vaenga. On 7 March Sqn Ldr Furniss (BP917) and Flg Off E G Searle (BP926) set out from Sumburgh, in the Shetland Islands. Five hours later Searle touched down at Vaenga, but Furniss experienced engine trouble as he approached the Norwegian coast and had to force-land at Afrikanda, south of Murmansk. Back at Sumburgh, Flg Off Dixon (BP929) took off on the 8th and arrived at Vaenga without incident.

Flg Off Searle (BP926) carried out the detachment's first successful sortie on 12 March when he obtained photographs of *Tirpitz* in Kåfjord from 28,000 ft. The Royal Navy planned its attack to take place on 4 April, and prior to this date nine sorties were flown to Altafjord by Spitfires, including two by the 3rd Aviation Squadron on 1 April. The attack achieved complete surprise, with large numbers of bombs striking the ship. On 26 May Searle took off on what was to prove the last, and most unorthodox, sortie of the detachment. Leaving Vaenga in BP926 at 2350 hrs, he flew to Altafjord and by the light of the midnight sun successfully photographed *Tirpitz* before landing back at Vaenga at 0220 hrs on the 27th.

Shortly after this sortie, word was received that the detachment was to return to Britain, and the two remaining Spitfires, BP926 and BP929, where handed over to the 3rd Aviation Squadron. By the start of June the Soviet unit recorded a total of four Spitfire PR IVs on strength, but a further loss occurred on the 18th when BP926, flown by Stárshiy Leytenánt I Y Popovich, was shot down as he attempted to cover Kirkenes.

The surviving Spitfires of the 3rd Aviation Squadron were tasked with obtaining coverage of *Tirpitz* in Kåfjord during August and September in the lead up to Operation *Paravane* – the attack on the vessel by RAF heavy bombers based at Yagodnik, in northwest Russia. They were also heavily involved with covering German airfields, strong points and ports in preparation for the Petsamo–Kirkenes offensive that took place in October, and in the subsequent liberation of the Finnmark region. Despite the limited numbers of aircraft available, the Soviets were able to utilise the Spitfire's performance to obtain vitally important photographic coverage that made a great contribution to the Allied war effort in the Arctic.

As the *Tungsten* detachment soldiered on with its veteran PR IVs, the last wartime PR version of the Spitfire was about to arrive at Benson. For some time work had been ongoing with the development of a PR variant of the Spitfire F XIV. The PR XIX retained the basic airframe of the F XIV, but like previous reconnaissance versions, it used the 'D' wing which incorporated leading edge fuel tanks. The PR XIX was fitted with the Griffon 65 engine that powered a five-bladed Rotol propeller. The internal fuel capacity of the Griffon 65-equipped aircraft was 217 gallons, which could be supplemented by a single under-fuselage slipper tank of various capacities.

Although the first 25 PR XIXs produced were unpressurised, the remainder all featured a pressure cabin. Another feature of the pressurised version was the addition of an extra 20-gallon fuel tank in each wing for a total internal fuel capacity of 257 gallons. The safe range of the PR XIX was 950 miles on internal fuel, which was increased to 1160 miles with the addition of the extra wing tanks of the pressurised version. Its service ceiling was rated at 42,500 ft, but in reality the aircraft was easily capable of exceeding 45,000 ft.

The power of the Griffon engine made the PR XIX exceedingly fast, with a speed advantage of approximately 20 mph over the PR XI at most altitudes. The cockpit was fitted with a bulged Lobelle sliding canopy hood, and the armoured windscreen retained on the PR X was replaced with a frameless and strengthened plain windscreen. The PR XIX featured the 'U' type camera installation, and for tactical work a forward-facing oblique F24 camera could be installed in each wing. In total, 225 PR XIXs were produced.

The first two examples of the unpressurised PR XIX, RM627 and RM628, arrived at Benson on 30 April 1944, with the latter aircraft being passed on to No 542 Sqn during May. The first PR XIX sortie was carried out on 24 May by No 542 Sqn's Sqn Ldr Ball (RM628), who obtained photographs of coastal targets in the Le Havre area. On 15 June No 541 Sqn's Sqn Ldr J H Saffery (RM633) was tasked with objectives in the Ruhr, but was forced to abandon his aircraft over the Channel when its engine failed. RM633 was the first PR XIX to be lost on operations, although Saffery was rescued.

The anticipated V1 flying bomb offensive had commenced just 48 hours before the loss of RM633, with a number of weapons being fired at London. From then on, the search for launch sites became an even higher priority for No 106(PR) Group, with Allied attacks to destroy them being stepped up. This in turn generated ever greater demands for D/A, particularly from low-level. Ironically, no dedicated low-level version of the PR Spitfire remained in service, with the PR XIII having long been retired from the inventories of Nos 541 and 542 Sqns.

June proved to be an exceptionally busy month for No 542 Sqn, with a record 226 operational sorties carried out. Whilst the majority were flown in the PR XI, both the PR X and PR XIX made useful

Spitfire PR XIX RM633 of No 541 Sqn was photographed in early June 1944 shortly after joining the unit. Although the first operational PR XIX sortie was flown on 24 May by No 542 Sqn, the type was not cleared for general use until the following month. RM633 was lost on its first operational sortie on 15 June. Sqn Ldr John Saffery had been tasked with photographing targets in the Ruhr, but as he crossed the Channel his oil pressure dropped to zero and his propeller stuck in fine pitch. Forced to glide back to the English coast, he eventually had to bail out due to rapid altitude loss. Despite an extensive ASR effort Saffery was not found until night had fallen, when he was picked up by a MTB heading out to patrol off the Belgian coast (*Author's Collection*)

contributions. For No 541 Sqn, the weather had a much greater impact on flying, with the conditions over northern and central Germany restricting operations for much of the month. The crash of RM633 was the only operational Spitfire loss suffered by No 106(PR) Group during June, but the 14th PRS at Mount Farm had not been so lucky. On the 15th Lt R W Diderickson (PL790) was tasked with covering objectives in the Évreux and Coulommiers areas, but he crashed near Paris, whilst on the 28th Maj C T Haugen (PL767) was killed when his PR XI crashed near Watlington, in Oxfordshire, in poor weather as he returned from covering the Paris area.

Towards the end of July an ominous threat made its first appearance in the skies over Germany when a No 544 Sqn Mosquito was intercepted by a jet fighter in the Munich area. This was the first known encounter with a Me 262, but No 106(PR) Group had already run into the rocket-powered Me 163 back on 29 May when No 542 Sqn's Flt Lt G R Crakanthorp (MB791) was tasked with photographing the German North Sea ports;

'After covering Wilhelmshaven, I observed an aircraft climbing rapidly at about 3000 ft per minute. I climbed as soon as I saw him, and as I reached 41,000 ft he was only 1000 yards to the south of me, but still a few thousand feet below. As I readied to turn into his attack, the exhaust plume on his aircraft stopped and he turned away without gaining any more height.'

Crakanthorp had encountered a Me 163 of *Erprobungskommando* 16, based at Bad Zwischenahn, which had started combat trials earlier that month. Fortunately for him, Crakanthorp had been intercepted at the limit of the rocket fighter's endurance, and the extra altitude gained probably saved his life.

By the end of August much of France was in Allied hands, with Paris having been liberated on the 25th. Although Luftwaffe opposition over France was minimal, an increasing number of Mosquitos were being intercepted over southern Germany by Me 262s. Such was the frequency that No 106(PR) Group urgently argued that Spitfire PR XIXs should be used wherever possible to relieve the Mosquitos. Until such time as the PR XIX had the range to operate over southern Germany, it was proposed that aircraft flying from Italy take over responsibility for the Munich area.

During the summer of 1944 PR XI EN664 'Q' *BRENDA* was regularly flown by Flg Off John Bendixsen of No 541 Sqn's 'B' Flight at St Eval. Its last operational sortie from the Cornish base was undertaken on 14 July 1944 when, despite being subjected to much light flak, Bendixsen successfully covered the RDF station at Le Conquet at low level (*Author's Collection*)

It was during August that No 106(PR) Group received notification that production of the PR XI was to be phased out from December 1944, and that all Spitfire PR squadrons would have their PR XIX establishment increased.

The start of September saw the Allied armies in France make spectacular advances. Many of the flying bomb launch sites in the Pas-de-Calais were overrun, effectively halting the campaign against Britain and thus ending a major commitment for British-based strategic reconnaissance aircraft. Between May and September, PR had located 133 modified V1 launch sites in northern France, allowing the threat to be largely neutralised by aerial bombing. All told, more than 3000 PR sorties had been flown in connection with the flying bomb campaign since 1943, the majority by the Spitfires of Nos 541 and 542 Sqns, along with a significant contribution from the 14th PRS.

With German resistance seemingly on the edge of collapsing, the Allies hastily set about preparing for an airborne operation to capture bridges across the Rhine. On 6 September No 541 Sqn flew 16 sorties, of which eight attempted to cover bridges across the Meuse/Maas, Waal and Rhine between Grave and Arnhem. Three were carried out at low-level by PR XIXs fitted with a new forward-facing oblique F24 camera installation.

The original plan to seize the Rhine bridges was expanded into a major operation involving most of the First Allied Airborne Army. No 106(PR) Group was called upon to provide the bulk of the photographic coverage for the new operation, now known as *Market Garden*. Once it began on 17 September, No 541 Sqn continued to generate photographic coverage, with the busiest day being the 19th when six successful sorties were flown to Arnhem. Despite six days of heavy fighting, *Market Garden* was a costly failure, with the Germans managing to prevent an Allied breakthrough.

In the meantime, No 542 Sqn endeavoured to penetrate deeper and deeper into central and southern Germany in an effort to relieve Mosquitos of the duty. While September had resulted in the loss of three USAAF Spitfires, it looked likely Nos 541 and 542 Sqns would see the month out without casualties. Unfortunately this was not to be, for on the 28th Flt Lt D K McCuaig (PL904) of No 541 Sqn failed to return from a sortie to Bremen. He had been intercepted and shot down by a Fw 190D-9 southwest of the city, McCuaig's PR XI being the first to fall to the new Focke-Wulf fighter.

The failure of *Market Garden* effectively ended major ground operations in the west for the remainder of 1944. However, the Combined Bombing Offensive against German industrial targets had resumed after a brief hiatus caused by *Overlord*, with attacks now being stepped up against oil installations.

With the liberation of most of France and Belgium, an increasing amount of the work of the Spitfires based at Benson and Mount Farm was connected with the various aspects of the bombing offensive. By the middle of October it was proposed that Nos 541 and 542 Sqns would be equipped with 15 PR XIXs and five PR XIs each. It was anticipated that a pressurised version of the PR XIX would soon be in limited production, with full production scheduled for February 1945.

At the start of December, No 541 Sqn was informed that it would be required to provide a detachment to the Continent in support of the First

Allied Airborne Army to assist in gathering intelligence in preparation for further airborne landings. On the 15th, three Spitfires (PR X MD198, PR XI PA859 and PR XIX RM637) left Benson for Brussels/Melsbroek (B58). Due to poor weather, it was not until the 23rd that the detachment undertook its first sorties, with Flg Off C K Arnold (RM637) photographing the Wesel area and Flt Lt G E Walker (PA959) covering Emmerich.

On New Year's Day the Luftwaffe launched Operation *Bodenplatte*, which saw fighters from 34 *Jagdgruppen* attack Allied airfields in Belgium, the Netherlands and France. Brussels/Melsbroek was attacked early in the morning, with heavy damage inflicted on numerous reconnaissance aircraft belonging to the 2nd TAF as Bf 109s and Fw 190s made repeated strafing passes. The No 541 Sqn detachment did not escape unscathed, with MD198 being totally destroyed and PA859 badly damaged. The detachment ended shortly after *Bodenplatte*, with the three aircraft having gathered much detailed information that SHAEF and the First Allied Airborne Army would soon put to good use.

Back in Britain, the 7th PG(R) flew its 4000th sortie on 24 February 1945, the honour falling to a PR XI flown by Lt J H Roberts of the 14th PRS who successfully covered targets around Leipzig.

By the beginning of March, German resistance west of the Rhine had almost been eliminated. In the air, the relentless campaign against the enemy's oil and transportation targets continued unabated, with constant requests for targeting and D/A keeping all PR units busy.

March was also marked by the high number of interceptions made by Luftwaffe fighters, particularly jet- and rocket-powered machines. On the 3rd, No 541 Sqn's Flg Off W G Brooks was assigned oil targets in the Aschersleben and Böhlen areas, but he was killed when his PR XI crashed. The following day the unit suffered another loss when Flt Lt Scargill was forced to bail out of his PR XIX on a D/A sortie to Bielefeld. On the 9th, Flt Lt G Platts went missing in PR XIX RM631 on a sortie to cover airfields in the Hanover area, and ten days later PR XI PL856 flown by

In early 1945 some of the Spitfire PR XIs flown by the 14th PRS exchanged their PRU Blue camouflage scheme for a natural metal finish. By this time all of the squadron's aircraft were identified by an Olive Green rudder, and they were also marked with the red identification bar of the 7th PG(R) on the engine cowling. PA892 served with the 14th PRS for 15 months before being handed back to the RAF on 3 April 1945 (*Author's Collection*)

Flt Lt B K L Fuge failed to return from a mission to targets between Lüneburg and Oranienburg. Finally, on the 21st, Flt Lt F P Adlam (RM635) was killed on a sortie to Hamburg, his aircraft being the third PR XIX lost by the squadron during the month.

Despite German resistance on the ground showing signs of breaking, the level of interception by the Luftwaffe against reconnaissance aircraft had been unprecedented. Indeed, the casualties incurred by No 541 Sqn in March were the highest suffered by the unit during the war. For the month as a whole No 541 Sqn had flown 168 sorties, but the cost had been high, with five pilots missing. Likewise, No 542 Sqn had been extremely busy, with the unit flying 130 operational sorties, but fortunately it had escaped without any casualties. At Mount Farm, the 14th PRS had also avoided losses, despite flying many sorties.

As it appeared the war in Europe was nearing its end, USAAF planners began preparing for the transfer of the Eighth Air Force to the Pacific. As part of these plans, all units would be equipped with American aircraft, and as such, on 29 March, the 14th PRS was informed that it would be swapping its Spitfires for F-5 Lightnings. In the 17 months the Spitfire had served with the 7th PG(R), the aircraft had earned a reputation for reliability and outstanding performance. For a long period the Spitfires of the 14th PRS were the only machines from the 7th PG(R) capable of securing the photographs necessary for the USAAF bomber force to continue its offensive against German targets.

By May much of the Third Reich was in Allied hands and PR operations had practically ceased. On the 7th Flg Off I H Seddon (PM189) of No 541 Sqn carried out his unit's last operational sortie of the war from Benson when he covered Flensburg and Kiel. Earlier that same day, No 542 Sqn's Flg Off K Durbidge (PA948) successfully completed his squadron's last mission when he covered the Biscay ports. Enemy forces unconditionally surrendered on 8 May.

One of the main factors contributing to the rapid collapse of German resistance was the systematic targeting of its oil industries. PR had enabled Allied interpreters to identify nearly all of Germany's oil refineries and storage facilities, and once a concerted effort was begun to destroy them output was severely impacted. Much of the credit for this success must go to the Spitfires of No 106(PR) Group and the 7th PG(R), which were often the only reconnaissance aircraft capable of operating in areas where German jets were active. Although it had been intended that the PR X and PR XI Spitfires of No 106(PR) Group would be replaced by the PR XIX during 1945, delays in production meant that the PR XI remained the main operational type with both Nos 541 and 542 Sqns through to VE Day.

With the cessation of hostilities in Europe, the PR squadrons at Benson were put on standby for the possibility of transferring to Southeast Asia. However, neither Nos 541 or 542 Sqns were required to move as Japan surrendered three months after Germany. Within days of the announcement, No 542 Sqn was disbanded (on 27 August 1945), but No 541 Sqn continued to operate Spitfire PR XIs and PR XIXs for survey work until it too was disbanded on 1 October 1946 and renumbered No 82 Sqn.

# CHAPTER FOUR

# IN SUPPORT OF THE ARMY

The disbandment of No 1 PRU in October 1942 made little difference to the day-to-day operations of No 140 Sqn, which continued to cover German coastal defences in France as part of RAF Army Co-operation Command's No 34 Wing. By the start of 1943, the unit's PR VIIs were old and worn, and even the performance of the PR IV was inferior to the latest German fighters. In February the War Office made a request for No 140 Sqn to be re-equipped with the Spitfire PR XI, but the limited numbers available meant that this was denied. On 12 March No 140 Sqn was informed that it would be moving to Hartford Bridge, in Hampshire, from where the first successful sortie was flown on the 16th when Flg Off E W Forwell (AB118) covered La Havre.

On 1 June 1943, RAF Army Co-operation Command was disbanded and replaced by the newly formed Tactical Air Force (TAF). It was intended that the new organisation would meet all the air support requirements of the 21st Army Group – the British component of the forces earmarked for the forthcoming invasion of northwest Europe. No 140 Sqn remained a part of No 34 Wing at Hartford Bridge, where it was joined by No 16 Sqn on the 29th. It was planned that the latter unit would convert to the Spitfire PR XI, and together with No 140 Sqn it would fulfil the PR demands of HQ TAF.

The amount of operational flying by No 140 Sqn during August dropped off significantly as the unit's Spitfires were used to convert

Spitfire PR XI EN654 was assigned to No 16 Sqn, which was the second PR unit to join No 34 Wing. It provided direct support to the 21st Army Group, the controlling HQ for British forces allocated for the invasion of northwest Europe. Once No 140 Sqn fully converted to the Mosquito in April 1944, No 16 Sqn became the sole PR Spitfire operator within the wing (*Author's Collection*)

Wg Cdr Eric Le Mesurier, CO of
No 140 Sqn, poses for the camera in the
cockpit of one of his unit's Spitfire PR VIIs.
Le Mesurier was one of the finest PR pilots
in the RAF, and was the first to be awarded
the Distinguished Service Order, in March
1941 – he had received a Distinguished
Flying Cross in May 1940. He was an early
member of the PDU and served with
No 212 Sqn in France, before being given
command of the PRU's 'C' Flight. Le
Mesurier then went on to form RAF Army
Co-operation Command's own dedicated
PRU, No 1416 Flight/No 140 Sqn, which he
commanded until mid-1943. He was killed
in a flying accident in a Mosquito T III whilst
serving as Chief Instructor of No 8(C) OTU
on 23 December 1943 (*Author's Collection*)

No 16 Sqn onto the type. Although No 140 Sqn had been informed it would be converting to the Mosquito, two new Spitfire PR XIs were received on 4 September. On the 8th Flg Off C Mason (EN681) flew the unit's first operational PR XI sortie when he successfully photographed targets in the Pas-de-Calais. No 16 Sqn was able to perform its first high-altitude PR sortie of the war in one of No 140 Sqn's PR XIs on the 18th when Flt Lt A N Davis flew EN680 to Boulogne, where he obtained photographs from 30,000 ft. On 8 November No 16 Sqn was finally allotted its own Spitfires when six PR IVs and two PR XIs were received from No 140 Sqn. These were quickly followed by eight new PR XIs delivered from Benson.

On the 15th, No 34 Wing's controlling HQ was re-designated 2nd TAF. In addition to No 34 Wing, which was directly sub-ordinate to HQ 2nd TAF, each army within the 21st Army Group was allocated a reconnaissance wing to meets its own demands. The Canadian First Army was supported by No 35 Wing and the British Second Army's needs would be met by No 39 Wing. It was intended that each wing would consist of one PR squadron, with one flight of Spitfires and one of Mosquitos, and two or more Tac/R squadrons equipped with the Mustang I.

Within No 35 Wing, No 4 Sqn was chosen to become a photographic unit, whereas within No 39 Wing, the Royal Canadian Air Force's No 400 Sqn was selected for the role. Towards the end of November, No 400 Sqn received its first two Spitfires, both PR XIIIs, for training. No 4 Sqn was informed that its 'A' Flight would re-equip with the Spitfire PR XI, although this was delayed by a number of weeks due to a shortage of machines. As an interim measure, three Spitfire PR XIIIs were received on 30 December.

A number of the sorties flown by Nos 140 and 16 Sqns at the end of December were in connection with covering *Crossbow* sites. Earlier in the month, the Allies had commenced large-scale *Noball* attacks on these locations, with the JIC requesting that 2nd TAF assist with photography. The PR Spitfires tasked with undertaking these missions would continue to play a significant part in the campaign against the *Crossbow* sites until they moved to the Continent following the invasion.

Over the course of 1943 the reconnaissance squadrons allocated to support the invasion forces had seen great change. For Nos 16, 4 and 400 Sqns, it meant switching to a new role and re-equipment, and at the turn of the year only No 16 Sqn was operational with Spitfires. No 140 Sqn had finally received PR XIs, but not before being informed it would be giving up all of its Spitfires for Mosquitos.

It was no secret that the invasion of Europe was likely to take place in the late spring or early summer of 1944, and from March onwards the pressure of work on 2nd TAF's reconnaissance squadrons increased rapidly with greater demand for coverage of targets in Normandy and the Pas-de-Calais. Unfortunately, No 16 Sqn incurred its first operational loss of a PR XI on

8 March when Flg Off A L Pearsall (PA863) failed to return from a sortie to Calais.

At the start of 1944 both Nos 400 and 4 Sqns were busy training and building up their strength. On 19 January, No 400 Sqn received its first two PR XIs. The unit's first operational PR XI sortie was carried out on 9 February when Sqn Ldr R A Ellis (PA886) photographed *Noball* targets in the Pas-de-Calais. No 4 Sqn received its first PR XI on 14 January, and the aircraft made its operational debut on 7 March when Flt Lt D A Draper (PA857) attempted to cover *Noball* sites.

With the invasion of Europe imminent, 2nd TAF's PRUs were fully occupied with tasks over the Continent. However, with the exception of No 16 Sqn, they were hampered by re-equipment – No 140 Sqn was winding down its Spitfire operations and Nos 4 and 400 Sqns were experiencing problems introducing the Mosquito into service. In contrast, the PR XI had proven a great success, and it now fell to No 16 Sqn and the Spitfire-equipped flights of Nos 4 and 400 Sqns to fulfil the majority of 2nd TAF's burgeoning photographic demands.

Flg Off Peter Brearley of No 140 Sqn stands in front of one of the unit's Spitfire PR XIs at Hartford Bridge. He had joined No 140 Sqn in November 1942 after completing his training at No 8(C) OTU. Brearley carried out the squadron's very last Spitfire sortie in PR XI EN663 on 27 April 1944 when he successfully covered targets between Port-en-Bessin-Huppain and Carentan, in Normandy (*Author's Collection*)

April saw No 140 Sqn fly more than 100 sorties, but only three were carried out in Spitfires. The unit's very last PR XI sortie was conducted on the 27th by Flg Off P G Brearley (EN663) when he obtained photographs of Carentan. The unit had been equipped with Spitfires since its formation in March 1941, and for many on the squadron it was a sad day, including Brearley;

'As a photo-recce pilot in a Spitfire, there was a high workload – you had to navigate and look out for the enemy. If you were attacked in a Spit you could nearly always get out of trouble, especially with the PR XI. I was sorry to see the Spitfires go.'

On 10 April, No 4 Sqn flew six sorties to cover *Noball* sites and rivers in northern France and Belgium. Five of these were conducted in Spitfires, and unfortunately included the squadron's first operational loss on the type. Flg Off I A Turnbull (PA901) was briefed to photograph canals in the Knocke-Hulst area but failed to return.

At the start of May, both Nos 4 and 400 Sqns were notified that they would be losing their Mosquitos and would fully equip with the Spitfire, which offered improved serviceability and was much better suited to the shorter range, high frequency work carried out by the units. On the 3rd they were officially informed that their establishments would change to 18 Spitfire PR XIs.

During the last ten days of May a concerted campaign was begun to destroy the German radar network along the north coast of France from Brittany to the Pas-de-Calais. All of 2nd TAF's PRUs were heavily tasked with obtaining D/A photographs and monitoring German efforts to repair their installations. By the time of the invasion not one single station was left fully functional, with much credit for this going to the PR organisation and the squadrons of 2nd TAF.

On 27 May Flt Lt P O Miles (PA929) carried out No 16 Sqn's first low-level Spitfire sortie when he successfully covered the coast between Berck-sur-Mer and Cayeux-sur-Mer, his aircraft being fitted with split F52 moving film cameras.

## OVERLORD

Nine days later all of 2nd TAF's aircraft were painted with invasion stripes ready for D-Day operations on 6 June. Once the landings began, it was intended that each army would be directly supported by its own reconnaissance wing. The Tac/R squadrons supporting each army would provide visual intelligence and some oblique photography, whereas each wings' PR squadron would be responsible for photography up to a range of about 150 miles. Beyond this, No 34 Wing would secure intelligence for HQ 21st Army Group to a depth of 300 miles, with No 16 Sqn now being the sole operator of PR Spitfires in the wing.

As D-Day dawned the weather quickly deteriorated, with No 400 Sqn only flying three sorties on the 6th and No 4 Sqn just a single mission. No 16 Sqn was able to despatch the most aircraft, with 16 sorties attempted, although most failed to secure any photographs.

In keeping with the policy of conducting low-level operations, which were now being more frequently undertaken, No 16 Sqn took delivery of six Spitfire IXs on 18 June. These were standard F IXs which retained their armament and normal fuel configuration, but were modified to carry a single port-facing oblique F24 camera. Known as the FR IX, the aircraft flown by No 16 Sqn were painted in the pale pink scheme first seen on No 1 PRU Spitfires in 1941. The FR IX was only produced in limited numbers, with most being used in northwest Europe. Sqn Ldr E M Goodale undertook his unit's first sortie in the type on the 23rd when he successfully covered rail targets around Saint-Omer.

On the first day of July, No 400 Sqn's 'A' Flight flew its nine PR XIs to Sommervieu (B8) near Bayeux in order to rapidly respond to Army requests. The first PR operations were flown from B8 on the 3rd when six sorties were sent to targets around Caen. On the 17th the unit suffered its first operational PR XI loss when Flt Lt F E Hanton was forced to abandon PA797 when his engine caught fire on a sortie to Villers-Bocage. He was able to bail out near Bayeux as he tried to return to B8, but suffered burns. At the end of July No 4 Sqn began operating a two-aircraft detachment from within the beachhead at Plumetot (B10). On the 31st, Flt Lt Draper and Flg Off A R Hutchinson flew to France, ready to begin operations the following day.

August brought no let up in air operations as the fighting in Normandy was reaching a critical stage. On the first day of the month No 16 Sqn was heavily committed to targets in northeast France, with nine sorties being flown. Flt Lt A P G Holden twice encountered Fw 190s as he attempted to cover bridges across the River Eure, but in both cases the superior performance of his PR XI got him out of trouble.

At the start of August the Americans had succeeded in breaking out of the western end of the beachhead and quickly overran Brittany. In the following week they swung round to the north and threatened to trap

German forces in a large salient centred on Falaise. By the 21st the pocket was sealed and the bulk of the German Seventh Army destroyed. From this point on enemy resistance in northern France was effectively over and a full-scale retreat east began. This situation had been anticipated by the 21st Army Group, with No 16 Sqn having already flown numerous sorties to all the major communications centres in northeastern France and Belgium.

The intense fighting south of Caen in August meant that No 400 Sqn was called on to fulfil numerous demands in the area. On the 4th the unit flew 16 sorties from B8, with 12 obtaining photographs of their objectives. During the evening of the 10th 'B' Flight reunited with the rest of the squadron when it transferred to France. On 15 August the whole squadron made the first of many moves when it transferred to Sainte-Honorine-de-Ducy (B21). Operations were not disrupted, however, continuing throughout the day.

On 1 August, No 4 Sqn carried out its first operation from within the beachhead when Flt Lt Draper (PA852) was tasked with searching for a rail gun. The pilot obtained photographs of the railway lines between Argentan and Caen from 12,000 ft, and when Draper's images were examined the interpreters located the gun, allowing it to be attacked by Typhoons. On the 16th the remainder of No 4 Sqn transferred to Bény-sur-Mer (B4), where, on arrival the pilots found the detachment from B10 already set up. Operations commenced the next day.

Due to the rapid retreat of the Germans towards the Seine, sorties were flown further to the east, and on 25 August No 4 Sqn set a new record when 32 sorties were generated. It had, in fact, been a busy month for all of 2nd TAF's PRUs, with every squadron flying well over 200 sorties.

By mid-September, the frontlines had stabilised as the Germans consolidated their positions along the Siegfried Line and in southern Holland along the Scheldt and Maas. The enemy had left strong garrisons in most of the Channel Ports to deny their use to the Allies, and they also controlled both banks of the Scheldt Estuary, which made Antwerp useless as a port.

On 4 September, No 16 Sqn began transferring to Balleroy (A12) in the American sector, southwest of Bayeux. Its first operations were flown from the airfield the following day when seven PR XI sorties were sent to the

A Spitfire PR XI of No 400 Sqn taxis across the grass at Sainte-Honorine-de-Ducy (B21) in late August 1944. When the unit transferred here from Sommervieu (B8) on 15 August, operations were not disrupted in any way. Indeed, by 1000 hrs all 18 of No 400 Sqn's PR XIs had either flown directly to B21 or taken off from B8 on operations and landed at the new base upon their return. The PRUs of 2nd TAF tried to stay in close proximity to the HQs issuing photographic demands, as this greatly expedited the despatch of aircraft and the processing and analysis of the intelligence gained (*Author's Collection*)

Netherlands, eastern France and the lower Rhine districts of Germany. On the 9th the squadron was ordered to move to Amiens/Glisy (B48), with the aircraft transferring during the morning. Two sorties were flown from B48 in the afternoon, with WO W J Willshaw bringing back photographs of the mouth of the Elbe. Flg Off J Wallace failed to return from a mission to the Netherlands, however.

On 10 September an earlier Allied plan to cross the lower Rhine was expanded into an even bigger operation involving the whole of the First Allied Airborne Army. As previously noted, the original aim of *Market Garden* was the capture of bridges over the river, but the operation now called for the near simultaneous insertion of three parachute divisions. Although the ground elements for the operation would come from the 21st Army Group, PR in the lead-up period was largely undertaken by No 106(PR) Group.

On 16 September, Wg Cdr Webb from No 34 Wing, together with Flg Offs G A Winter, L L Cadan and J R Brodby of No 16 Sqn, flew back to Northolt, where their Spitfires would be available to fulfil photographic demands originating directly from HQ First Allied Airborne Army once the airborne landings began. The first sortie was undertaken the following day by Wg Cdr Webb when he covered bridges and drop zones at Arnhem, Nijmegen and Eindhoven at low level in PR XI PL834.

On the ground, the Germans managed to clear British paratroopers from the centre of Arnhem, and although fighting continued for a number of days *Market Garden* had effectively failed. The operation had expended most of the supplies available in France, as Allied forces were then still very much dependent on over-extended logistical routes. Failure to clear the Channel Ports or the Scheldt Estuary meant an enforced end to offensive operations along most of the front. This pause enabled many of 2nd TAF's units to move nearer to the front, including No 34 Wing. On 27 September, No 16 Sqn moved 120 miles northeast to Melsbroek (B58), near Brussels. The next day eight sorties were flown to targets in the Netherlands and Germany, with all bringing back photographs. It had been a tough month for the squadron, which had lost four pilots killed or missing – its worst level of casualties since becoming a PR unit.

At the start of September No 400 Sqn was again on the move, this time to Avrilly (B34), near Évreux in France. Twelve sorties were flown on the 4th, including eight in the evening to German targets. Flt Lt L W Seath (PL837) was tasked with obtaining photographs to form a mosaic of the Osnabrück area. He landed back at B34 in darkness with 15 gallons of fuel remaining after 4 hr 9 min flying time. This was the longest sortie yet flown by the squadron, and the deepest penetration into Germany. On 20 September the squadron moved to Blankenberge (B66), in Belgium, to bring it closer to the British Second Army frontline, but little operational flying was possible for the remainder of September. Despite this, No 400 Sqn had flown

Sqn Ldr Charles Harris-St John took over command of No 4 Sqn from Wg Cdr Robert Hardiman in May 1944, and he subsequently led it until the unit was disbanded in August 1945. He flew his first sortie with No 4 Sqn on 25 May 1944 when he covered targets in the Neufchâtel, Honfleur and Le Havre areas. Harris-St John is seen as a pilot officer in the cockpit of a Type G Spitfire of No 140 Sqn, with whom he completed a long tour during which he was awarded a DFC (for a harrowing flight over Dieppe on 18 August 1942) and Bar (*Author's Collection*)

246 operational sorties during the month and, more importantly, had not lost any pilots.

September had also seen No 4 Sqn make multiple moves before ending up at Saint-Denis-Westrem (B61), near Ghent in Belgium, on the 27th. This move brought No 35 Wing and its sub-ordinate units within 25 miles of the frontline, putting them in a good position to rapidly react to the reconnaissance demands of the Canadian First Army.

By the start of October Boulogne and Calais had been cleared of German defenders, but the port facilities were wrecked and, in any event, they lacked the capacity to meet the supply needs of all Allied armies in France. Only one port was capable of fulfilling this requirement and that was Antwerp, which was already in Allied hands. However, the shipping approaches through the Scheldt were still firmly under German control. Allied armies would not be able to resume full-scale offensive operations until their logistics issues were resolved, and as such they set about clearing the Germans from both banks of the Scheldt Estuary in what became known as the Battle of the Scheldt.

Reconnaissance operations by 2nd TAF's PRUs settled down into a series of generally routine sorties as the sectors in front of each army remained more or less stable. Monitoring German positions along the Scheldt remained one of the primary tasks of No 4 Sqn, together with regular coverage of western and central Holland. On 11 October the unit was on the move again, this time to Deurne (B70) near Antwerp. As was now standard practice, pilots took off from their old base and after completing their sorties recovered to the new location. Moving base was now a well-established routine and had little impact on operational efficiency, and the next day the squadron was able to carry out 22 Spitfire sorties.

Once the Scheldt had been cleared No 4 Sqn could concentrate on tasks further to the north behind the Maas and the Lek and into Germany, and for the remainder of the year this section of the frontline was relatively quiet. On 4 November Flt Lt E J Lischke (PA852) was detailed to cover targets west of Münster. As he neared his objectives, two Fw 190Ds attacked from the port quarter. The pilot immediately broke into them and made a tight climbing turn. To Lischke's dismay, the enemy aircraft were able to match his climb and stayed with him up to 36,000 ft. Just when it looked like the Focke-Wulf fighters were about to get into firing position, four USAAF Mustangs appeared and caused the enemy aircraft to break away.

On the 6th, Flt Lt R M Cowell attempted to cover targets in the Enschede area, but south of Hengelo he spotted an aircraft high above him. It closed rapidly and dived to attack. As it neared, Cowell could see it was a twin-engined jet, probably a Me 262. It opened fire from about 1000 yards, but as the range decreased the Spitfire pilot turned sharply into his assailant and it flashed by. Undeterred, the German aircraft made four more attacks, and each time Cowell successfully repeated his manoeuvre, preventing the jet from bringing its guns to bear. After the fifth attack Cowell was able to find refuge in cloud and the jet was not seen again.

On 23 November No 4 Sqn moved to Gilze-Rijen (B77) near Tilburg, in the Netherlands. This would be its last move for some time, and the unit settled down to a regular routine, with operations attempted whenever the weather permitted.

Spitfire PR XI PL883 of No 400 Sqn taxis towards the runway at a waterlogged Eindhoven (B78), the unit having moved here from Blankenberg (B66) on 3 October 1944. Due to the relative stability of the frontlines, it remained at the airfield until 7 March 1945. PL883 was one of the five PR XIs lost by No 400 Sqn during the Luftwaffe attack on B78 on New Year's Day 1945 (*Author's Collection*)

No 400 Sqn was also frequently on the move. On 3 October its 18 Spitfires had transferred from Blankenberge to Eindhoven (B78), in the Netherlands, from where the unit lost its first pilot on operations since converting to PR Spitfires. On the 28th Flt Lt W W Kennedy (PL925) took off on his second sortie of the day, this time tasked with covering targets between the Dutch border and Hamm, in Germany. It seems likely he was hit by flak near Arnhem, as his aircraft crashed near Steenderen with Kennedy still at the controls.

As Nos 4 and 400 Sqns concentrated on covering their respective sectors of the front, No 16 Sqn continued to range deeper into enemy territory, where encounters with Luftwaffe fighters were becoming more frequent. Increasing numbers of pilots were reporting sightings of German jets, but for the most part as long as the enemy were seen first they could be avoided. On 18 November seven sorties were sent to targets in the Netherlands and Germany, and one of these resulted in yet another loss for No 16 Sqn when Plt Off W C Heath failed to return from a low-level mission to photograph the bridges at Venlo, in the Netherlands.

By December the frontline in the Netherlands was more or less static, with the main area of fighting being around the German bridgehead across the Maas. Other than the 3rd, which allowed Nos 16 Sqn and 400 Sqns to fly 12 and 15 sorties, respectively, the weather for the first three weeks of the month prevented much operational flying by any of 2nd TAF's PRUs.

Within No 34 Wing the advent of the Me 262 had made No 140 Sqn's Mosquitos too vulnerable for daylight operations. Going forward, HQ 21st Army Group's daylight PR requirements would be met solely by the Spitfires of No 16 Sqn.

On 16 December the Germans began their Ardennes offensive, with the aim of retaking Antwerp. A period of poor weather had allowed the Wehrmacht to move its forces up to the front undetected by aerial reconnaissance. The PRUs of 2nd TAF, which had been practically grounded for a week, were all able to fly multiple sorties on the 23rd, with No 4 Sqn carrying out 18 successful operations. This tempo was maintained on Christmas Eve, with No 16 Sqn attempting 13 sorties.

As 1944 came to an end, the PR squadrons of 2nd TAF had flown many successful sorties in support of the 21st Army Group, which had been fighting in Europe since D-Day. Despite often difficult conditions, all units were always on standby to obtain aerial imagery.

## BODENPLATTE

1 January 1945 saw the Germans launch the last major Luftwaffe offensive of the war – Operation *Bodenplatte* – in an attempt to destroy Allied tactical air assets on the ground. At about 0900 hrs, the normal routine at Gilze-Rijen was interrupted by enemy fighters racing across the airfield at low-level. A number of Fw 190s and Bf 109s carried out strafing attacks, but damage to the airfield was minimal and none of No 4 Sqn's aircraft were hit. Further east, it was a different story at Eindhoven. For nearly 20 minutes German fighters made repeated attacks on the massed ranks of aircraft parked on the airfield dispersals. Five Spitfire PR XIs of No 400 Sqn were destroyed and another five badly damaged. Once the attack was over, the squadron was left with only three serviceable PR XIs.

One of No 16 Sqn's Spitfire PR XIs burns following the Luftwaffe's 1 January 1945 attack on Brussels/Melsbroek. No 34 Wing had a total of 18 aircraft destroyed during *Bodenplatte*, including three of No 16 Sqn's PR XIs (PL905, PL765 and PL766), although fortunately all of the unit's personnel escaped unscathed. Despite Melsbroek taking a beating, No 16 Sqn was still able to fly five successful sorties later that same day (*Author's Collection*)

Airfields all across Belgium and Holland were attacked more or less simultaneously. The reconnaissance aircraft of No 34 Wing at Melsbroek were hit particularly hard. For more than half an hour waves of fighters shot up aircraft and buildings, causing significant damage. During the course of the attack No 34 Wing lost 18 aircraft destroyed, including three Spitfire PR XIs from No 16 Sqn, with many more damaged. *Bodenplatte* had come as a complete surprise and destroyed and damaged many Allied aircraft and airfield facilities. However, most of the Allied units were back up to strength in a matter of days, and operations were hardly affected. For No 4 Sqn at Gilze-Rijen, the attack made little difference, with the unit despatching 21 sorties the same day. Although Melsbroek had taken a beating, No 16 Sqn was able to fly five sorties during the day, and even No 400 Sqn, which only had a handful of serviceable aircraft, flew three sorties.

After the excitement of the start of the month, air operations settled down into a more routine pattern. On the 14th, No 16 Sqn's Flg Off W F Barker was tasked with covering airfields east of the Ruhr, and near Düsseldorf he saw two aircraft climbing at high speed;

'I could see that they were Me 163s. The first attacked, and as I was turning ahead of him the other came out of the sun. I rolled into a dive, followed down by the second aircraft. At 3000 ft he was only about 200 yards behind and I started to pull out. The aircraft eventually started to level off but I blacked out. When I came to, I saw a cloud of grey smoke coming from the wood towards which I was diving. I think my pursuer was not able to pull up and went straight in.'

Barker was then able to return to base without further incident.

On 8 February the 21st Army Group began Operation *Veritable* to clear the Reichswald and drive the Germans from the area between the Maas and the Rhine. However, poor weather over the next few days prevented Nos 4 and 400 Sqns from carrying out many sorties. It was not until the 14th that a significant number of operations could be flown, with No 400 Sqn undertaking 15 sorties to the battle area. Likewise, No 4 Sqn flew a high number of sorties to the area of Goch–Wesel–Reichswald, with 21 of the 26 flown securing photographs. On the 21st No 4 Sqn set a new operational record by flying 40 sorties. Other than the large numbers of Allied aircraft observed, most sorties were largely uneventful, and were mainly to the battle area on the Canadian First Army's front between Weeze and Emmerich. By 5 March, the 21st Army Group had largely cleared the Germans from the west bank of the Rhine.

The success of *Veritable* meant another series of base moves for many of the units of 2nd TAF. On the 7th, No 39 Wing headed south to Petit Brogel (B90), near Peer in Belgium. The first operations by No 400 Sqn from here did not take place until the 9th, when four sorties were attempted to Wesel, Emmerich and the Ruhr, but all were unsuccessful due to cloud.

By 10 March, the Germans had withdrawn from the bridgehead at Wesel, destroying the last of the bridges across the Rhine just before they retreated. For weeks 2nd TAF's PRUs had been covering the Rhine, and now efforts were increased so that every yard of the eastern bank and the area beyond was photographed and examined.

On 17 March No 16 Sqn received its first examples of the Spitfire PR XIX from No 34 Wing Support Unit. Training began immediately, with pilots impressed by the PR XIX's power, although they found that the extra speed also made it less manoeuvrable compared to the PR XI. The first operational PR XIX sortie by the squadron was carried out on the 22nd by Flt Lt C Leigh-Murray (PS849) when he successfully covered targets north of the Ruhr and in the Dutch cities of Zutphen and Deventer from 27,000 ft.

Along the Canadian First Army's front, No 4 Sqn continued to provide good service, covering targets from Schouwen to Arnhem and deeper into

Wg Cdr Gordon Cole cruises over the clouds in Spitfire PR XI PA888 '4' of No 34 Wing Support Unit. The latter unit was formed to provide logistical support to No 34 Wing, with one of its main functions being to supply reserve pilots and aircraft to the wing's frontline units. In March 1945 Cole assumed command of the unit, having previously served as Wing Commander Operations with No 34 Wing. Prior to that he had flown PR Spitfires with No 2 PRU and No 680 Sqn in the Mediterranean *(Author's Collection)*

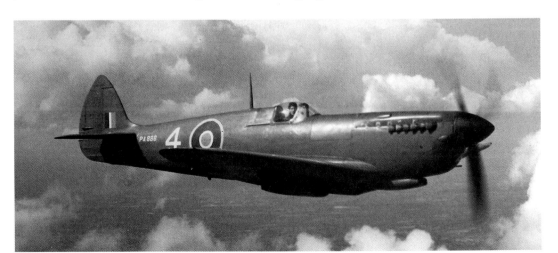

the Netherlands. In just a week the squadron flew more than 170 sorties, the vast majority of them being successful and without incident. On the 15th No 4 Sqn set another operational record by flying 43 successful sorties.

All of the aerial intelligence accumulated by 2nd TAF's PRUs, particularly that gathered by Nos 400 and 16 Sqns, was put to good use in planning the next phase of the advance into Germany. On the night of 23 March, the 21st Army Group would launch Operation *Plunder* to cross the River Rhine at Rees and Wesel. This would be followed up the next day by Operation *Varsity* – the largest single airborne operation ever attempted. All squadrons were able to fly numerous sorties on the day prior to the commencement of *Plunder* to obtain last minute photographs. By the 27th a substantial bridgehead had been established, and throughout this period all reconnaissance squadrons were very active as the weather conditions remained favourable.

27 March also saw No 16 Sqn receive official confirmation that its aircraft establishment had been changed from 18 Spitfire PR XIs to 18 PR XIXs, and by the end of March the unit had five PR XIXs on strength.

Once the Allied armies were across the Rhine, German resistance started to crumble. Reminiscent of the situation after the breakout from Normandy, the Allied advance was so rapid that headquarters were often unable to forecast their requirements for aerial reconnaissance as more and more territory was captured. One immediate dividend of the advance across the Rhine was the end of V2 launches against London and Antwerp. For many months the reconnaissance squadrons based on the Continent had searched in vain for the 'vengeance weapons', and despite almost daily sightings of vertical rocket trails, the launchers had remained elusive. Now this repetitive and ultimately futile task could be removed from the list of daily demands.

During April, No 16 Sqn continued to fly routine operations mainly to airfields in northwest Germany and targets in the Netherlands. On the 14th the unit transferred to Eindhoven, which would be the last wartime move undertaken by the squadron.

Due to the very fluid frontline and rapidly evolving situation, some of No 400 Sqn's sorties were tactical in nature, with pilots making visual reports to forward air controllers. On 10 April the unit moved to Rheine (B108), in Germany, but it was only there for six days before heading to Wunstorf (B116) near Hanover. By this time German forces had pulled back towards Bremen and Hamburg.

As No 400 Sqn was following closely behind the Allied advance into northern Germany, No 4 Sqn continued to support the Canadian First Army in its drive to isolate northern Holland. After a period of little flying, No 4 Sqn had a big day on the 7th when 36 sorties were conducted. All were to the northeast corner of the Netherlands, and all bar five were successful. On 17 April the squadron carried out 17 successful missions, but on completion of operations all aircraft transferred to Twente (B106), in the Netherlands, where the unit would stay for the remainder of hostilities in Europe.

By the middle of April the operational area was confined to northern Germany, Denmark and the Netherlands. Conventional PR missions were increasingly supplemented by calls for shipping reconnaissance in the coastal waters of the North Sea and the Baltic. For No 16 Sqn, this meant more sorties to targets in Denmark as the Germans shuttled vessels backwards and forwards between Norway.

Flt Lt Lawrence McMillan joined No 400 Sqn during April 1945 following a period of instructing in Canada. Prior to that, he had undertaken a long and very successful tour with No 542 Sqn at Benson. Ironically, he was killed on the first day of peace in Europe – 9 May 1945 – when his Spitfire PR XI was brought down by German flak whilst he was conducting a shipping reconnaissance mission off the coast of Denmark (*Author's Collection*)

The last really busy day for the squadron was on 25 April when 16 operations were flown. This included the unit's last Spitfire PR XIX sortie of the war, with Flt Lt J M Thompson (PS849) successfully covering Tönning and Sylt. All told, since No 16 Sqn had first received the PR XIX in March, only ten operational sorties had been undertaken with the type. By the time it entered service with the squadron, the PR XIX's superior performance was not really necessary as encounters with German aircraft were becoming rare. The unit's last operational sortie of the war was flown on 7 May. After covering multiple targets in Denmark at low-level, Flt Lt J Wheeler landed PR XI PL964 back at Eindhoven at 1845 hrs to bring No 16 Sqn's war to an end.

No 4 Sqn continued to fly a large number of sorties to the Netherlands and northwest Germany. The unit's final wartime mission was carried out on 8 May by Flt Lt P W Racey (PL793) when he successfully covered targets in the Rotenburg an der Wümme area in northern Germany.

The last days of hostilities in Europe saw No 400 Sqn flying an increasing number of sorties to cover German ports and shipping. On 3 May, instead of the usual high-level PR sorties, the unit began conducting medium- and low-level shipping reconnaissance missions flown by pairs of aircraft. Due to the surrender of enemy forces in northern Germany, all operations on the 21st Army Group's front ceased on the 5th, but the squadron continued to monitor shipping.

On 8 May No 400 Sqn was again on the move, this time to Lüneberg (B156). Here, word was received that the remaining enemy forces had surrendered, but due to the large numbers of vessels still approaching German and Danish ports, the squadron was still required to fly shipping patrols. Sadly, on one of these missions, the squadron incurred its first loss since October of the previous year. Flt Lts P G Wigle and L McMillan were detailed to carry out a shipping reconnaissance along the Great Belt, but only the former returned to Lüneberg;

'We observed four ships one mile off Spodsbjerg. I led the section down to deck level and passed within 100 yards of the vessels. I looked behind to observe my No 2 explode in mid-air. At the same time I observed machine gun strikes on the water between us. I immediately climbed and circled the position, but could only observe an oil slick on the water. It is my opinion that Flt Lt McMillan was killed outright.'

McMillan was flying PR XI PM142, and it is perhaps ironic that only the second Spitfire pilot loss suffered by the unit should have happened on the first official day of peace in Europe, and that it had been caused by enemy action.

With the end of the war in Europe, 2nd TAF's PRUs began to prepare for service against the Japanese. However, with the rapid end of the conflict in that theatre, all of the units equipped with PR Spitfires were deemed surplus to requirements and quickly disbanded. Nos 4, 16 and 400 Sqns, together with No 140 Sqn, had provided the forces earmarked for the invasion of Europe with the photographic intelligence they needed. In the lead-up to the invasion, this involved locating and monitoring all enemy defences along the coast. Once Allied forces were successfully ashore, they soon followed onto the Continent in order to fulfil the day-to-day tactical needs of the British and Canadian armies – a function they faithfully performed until Germany was defeated.

# CHAPTER FIVE

# OVERSEAS OPERATIONS

Long before Allied troops set foot back on the shores of Continental Europe, fighting had been raging in North Africa. By the start of 1943, the Allies had trapped Axis forces in Tunisia. The shrinking of enemy-held territory in North Africa had resulted in PR aircraft from three RAF commands operating over the same areas. This duly led to a review of the PR requirements for the Mediterranean theatre.

On 1 February 1943, No 2 PRU was re-designated No 680 Sqn, and on the same date No 4 PRU became No 682 Sqn, followed on 8 February by 'B' Flight of No 69 Sqn becoming No 683 Sqn. No 680 Sqn's 'A' Flight remained with No 285 Wing in support of the Eighth Army, which was consolidating its position on the Tunisian–Libyan frontier. The first sortie undertaken by the new 'A' Flight was carried out on 1 February when Plt Off L D O'Brien successfully covered sections of the Mareth Line.

Further to the west, No 682 Sqn was responsible for providing the bulk of the PR over Tunisia for the British First Army. On the 27th two Spitfires PR IXs were delivered from Britain, these aircraft being the first examples of the type to be received by the squadron.

On the island of Malta, PR became the responsibility of No 683 Sqn. The new unit's main tasks remained the monitoring of Axis ports and airfields in southern Italy and Sicily. On 16 February, Flt Lt M G Brown successfully covered Palermo and Trapani in EN153. This was the first ever sortie undertaken in the Mediterranean by a PR IX, EN153 having

Spitfire PR IV BP932 of No 683 Sqn has its engine tested at Luqa in February 1943, this aircraft having been delivered to 'B' Flight No 69 Sqn on Malta at the start of the year. On 22 February Flt Lt Malcolm Brown was tasked with covering Naples and ports in northwestern Sicily in BP932. His photographs revealed two cruisers and eight destroyers at Naples and a further 16 destroyers at Palermo and Trapani. On 7 March, after covering Naples and Palermo, Flt Sgt William Lewis overshot the runway whilst landing BP932 at Luqa and crashed into a quarry. Although the pilot survived the incident unscathed, the Spitfire was written off (*Author's Collection*)

Personnel from No 682 Sqn pose for a group photograph at Maison Blanche on 4 February 1943 – just four days after the unit had been formed from No 4 PRU. Note the skulls that adorned the unit's PR IVs during the early part of the campaign in Vichy French North Africa. Pilots seated in the front row (third from left to fourth from right) are Flt Sgt Bernard O'Connell, Flg Offs Harold Clyne and Roy Buchanan, Flt Lt Murray Anderson, Flg Offs Edwin Cowan and Daniel McKenzie and Sgt John Samson (*Author's Collection*)

reached No 683 Sqn on the 12th – the unit was the first outside of Britain to receive the type.

Problems with coordination between British and American forces resulted in the formation of Mediterranean Air Command (MAC) on 17 February to control all Allied air assets. In March, the Northwest African Photographic Reconnaissance Wing (NAPRW) was formed by bringing together No 682 Sqn and the USAAF's 3rd PG. The NAPRW would coordinate all PR operations by units based in French North Africa and would continue to fulfil the majority of demands over Tunisia.

Although the front in western Tunisia remained relatively static for much of March, there was no let up in activity for No 682 Sqn. On the 13th six successful sorties were carried out, including that flown by Flt Lt McKenzie, who covered Tunis and Bizerte in EN347. This was the first Spitfire PR XI mission undertaken overseas by the type, EN347 having been delivered to the unit on the 6th. On the 29th McKenzie (EN347) was tasked to cover Cagliari, but he was shot down by flak and killed. EN347 was the only PR XI on strength with No 682 Sqn, and its loss demonstrated that flying even the latest versions of the PR Spitfire was no guarantee of safety.

As the fighting in Tunisia entered its final stages, No 683 Sqn was busily engaged with covering objectives for the next phase of Allied operations – the invasion of Sicily. At the end of March the unit had received its first PR XI (EN338), which was flown on its first operation from Malta by Wg Cdr A Warburton when he successfully photographed Taranto and Crotone on 3 April.

In southern Tunisia No 680 Sqn was kept busy with photographic requests for the British Army. On 12 May, in what proved to be the last operational sortie flown over Tunisia by No 680 Sqn, Flg Off Barbour secured photographs of enemy gun batteries in the Enfidaville sector. The following day Axis forces surrendered. In its time in the Western Desert 'A' Flight No 2 PRU/No 680 Sqn had flown 687 sorties.

As reconnaissance aircraft set about trying to photograph every part of Sicily, the cover already obtained of the island of Pantelleria was about to be put to good use during an aerial bombing offensive codenamed Operation *Corkscrew*. No 683 Sqn's Flt Lt G H Maloney flew to the island on 15 May, where he successfully photographed Porto di Pantelleria and the airfield at Margana. In parallel with the attacks on Pantelleria, a concerted campaign was started to target Sicily and Sardinia, as well as transport infrastructure in Italy, in preparation for Operation *Husky* (the invasion of Sicily). Both Nos 682 and 683 Sqns would be heavily involved with securing the necessary photographs for the myriad raids conducted.

By the end of May air attacks on Sicily and Sardinia had intensified considerably, but the real focus of Allied air attacks was on Pantelleria. A constant watch was maintained on the island by No 683 Sqn, with each major raid followed up by a D/A sortie. On 11 June British troops landed on the island, and the defenders quickly surrendered. Much of the credit for the success enjoyed by the bombers in this short campaign must go to the PR organisation, with No 683 Sqn carrying out the majority of the operational tasks.

Ground personnel attempt to move a bogged Spitfire PR IV of No 680 Sqn's 'A' Flight in Libya. Heavy rains during early 1943 often turned the landing grounds into a sea of boggy, sandy mud that made take-offs and landings extremely hazardous, and even taxiing was next to impossible. In spite of the conditions, operational flying continued, although the results were often poor due to objectives being obscured by cloud (*Author's Collection*)

## EASTERN MED OPERATIONS

At the eastern end of the Mediterranean the remainder of the newly formed No 680 Sqn continued to keep a watch on Crete and the Dodecanese Islands. For the most part fighter opposition in the eastern Mediterranean was limited, but despite this there were other dangers. Mechanical failure was one such hazard, and Flg Off J Moss experienced this in PR IV BS362 on 12 February;

'When I was north of Rhodes at 33,000 ft my engine cut. I turned back towards the island, but it would not pick up. I was down to 10,000 ft, and by this time I had already attempted to bail out but my hood was jammed shut. I was so low that I thought I was going to crash into a snow-covered mountain, the top of which I only just cleared. The engine finally picked up enough to provide me with sufficient power to get home.'

Moss had been lucky, as operating over such large bodies of water meant practically no chance of rescue in an emergency.

February also saw No 680 Sqn lose its training commitment. Since the formation of No 2 PRU in 1941, the unit had always trained its own pilots. With the establishment of No 8(C) OTU in Britain in 1942, the training of PR aircrew was put on a more formal basis, although it was not until the restructuring and expansion of the whole PR organisation during the winter of 1942–43 that trained aircrew started to be posted overseas in significant numbers. Relieved of its training responsibilities, No 680 Sqn was ordered to transfer two pilots to No 74 OTU for PR instructor duties.

At the start of March 1943 No 680 Sqn had 14 PR IVs and two F VI/PRs on strength, the latter aircraft having arrived at the end of February from No 103 Maintenance Unit (MU). Following heavy PR Spitfire losses to Axis fighters over Crete at the end of 1942, requests were made to supply No 2 PRU with higher-performance machines.

As a stop-gap measure, No 103 MU modified high-altitude Spitfire F VI fighters for the PR role.

The F VI had been developed to counter the threat of high-flying German aircraft and featured a primitive pressure cockpit. In order to create an airtight seal, the rails for the canopy hood were removed and once the pilot was in the cockpit the hood was fixed in place by external fasteners. At No 103 MU all excess weight was removed and vertical F8 cameras installed in the rear fuselage, with three examples, BS106, BS133 and BS149, ultimately being sent to No 680 Sqn. Although these Spitfire F VI/PRs lacked the leading-edge wing tanks of the PR IV, they could carry a single drop tank.

It is not known what camouflage scheme was used on the F VI/PRs, but it is fair to assume that they sported Royal Blue in service with No 680 Sqn. However, by this time, not all of the unit's machines were camouflaged in this colour, as those arriving from Britain were in standard PRU Blue. The F VI/PR made its operational debut on 17 March when Flg Off R L Westinghouse (BS149) was tasked with covering the Greek port of Piraeus, although the mission was largely unsuccessful due to cloud. It was soon found that the performance of the F VI/PR was no better than that of the PR IV at high altitude, and whilst the pressure cockpit did alleviate some of the discomfort felt by pilots at extreme altitude, the fixed canopy was not popular and the variant was seldom used operationally.

With the return of No 680 Sqn's 'A' Flight from the Western Desert during June, preparations were made for 'B' Flight to operate as a permanent detachment from Derna and for 'C' Flight to do the same from Nicosia. Only 'A' Flight would remain at Kilo 8/Matariyah, in Egypt, where it would become the headquarters flight. By June 1943 the main focus was on *Husky*, with the majority of PR resources concentrated in the NAPRW, leaving No 680 Sqn comparatively little work.

The Allied plan for *Husky* called for simultaneous amphibious landings to be made by the US Seventh and British Eighth armies. By the date of the landings, which began on the night of 9–10 July, PR had provided the Allied commanders with a complete view of Axis dispositions in Sicily and southern Italy. In the lead up to the invasion No 682 Sqn maintained its watch on Sardinia, but on the day of the landings the unit flew its first mission to southern Italy when Sgt I P Morris covered targets in the Calabria region.

10 July also saw No 683 Sqn conduct eight Spitfire sorties to Sicily and southern Italy, all of which were flown in PR XIs. The unit flew an exceptional sortie on 16 August when Flg Off E C Hey covered the Naples area, with 28 separate pin-point targets photographed.

The last Axis troops were evacuated from Sicily on the 17th, bringing about an end to the battle for Sicily. Without doubt *Husky* was a major strategic success for the Allies, with the efforts of Nos 682 and 683 Sqns allowing a complete intelligence picture of enemy dispositions to be built up. On 26 August NAPRW took over responsibility for much of southern Italy. Prior to this, No 683 Sqn was responsible for covering targets as far north as Naples, but from this date onward the squadron's area of operations was limited to objectives in the Balkans and the 'toe' and 'heel' of Italy.

On 3 September Allied troops crossed the Straits of Messina and landed in Calabria during Operation *Baytown*. The beginning of the Italian

campaign called for the highest
degree of activity on the part
of MAC's PR organisation,
although for the most part
its aircraft were engaged in
routine tasks. On 9 September
the Allies made their main
landing at Salerno. Codenamed
Operation *Avalanche*, the US
Fifth Army was tasked with
seizing the port of Naples, but
was met with strong German
resistance. On the eve of

Spitfire PR XI EN657 of No 683 Sqn was
photographed at San Francesco, on Sicily,
in early August 1943, shortly after the unit
had started using the airfield – one of many
satellite landing grounds surrounding
Gerbini – as a forward base to fulfil British
Army demands for photographic coverage
of the island. The first two sorties from San
Francesco had been flown on 1 August,
with Plt Offs Durbidge and Craig both
successfully covering targets in the Catania
area (*Author's Collection*)

*Avalanche* the Italian government announced it had signed an armistice
with the Allies, although the Germans were able to stabilise the situation
in the country before the Allies could take full advantage.

With the surrender of the Italian fleet in southern Italy and the capture
of most of the territory in the region, there was now very little work left
for No 683 Sqn. It was duly informed that towards the end of the year it
would re-equip with the Mosquito. On 9 October the squadron ceased
operations over the Balkans and along the Adriatic coast, although from
the 20th it started to provide a single aircraft on a daily basis to undertake
PR flights for the US Fifth Army.

Although missions for No 683 Sqn practically stopped during October,
the same could not be said for No 682 Sqn, whose services with the
NAPRW were in high demand. Targeting and D/A of marshalling yards
and airfields for Allied bombers continued to make up the bulk of the
work. From 5 October the squadron's 'B' Flight was detached to Foggia,
where it joined No 285 Wing.

On the 26th, No 336(PR) Wing was formed to control RAF units
within the NAPRW. These included Spitfire-equipped No 682 Sqn and
No 60 Sqn of the South African Air Force (SAAF), which operated the
Mosquito. It was also intended to withdraw No 683 Sqn from Malta and
incorporate the unit into the new wing.

On 8 December, No 336(PR) Wing moved to San Severo, in Italy. With
the Allied lines now well north of Naples, it was considered desirable to
operate from the Italian mainland so as to greatly enhance the reach of the
wing's aircraft, particularly as more and more work was being conducted
in support of the strategic bombing offensive. On the 20th four pilots
from No 682 Sqn were transferred to No 683 Sqn, this representing a
change in policy with a reversal of the decision to re-equip the latter with
the Mosquito, which would now go to No 680 Sqn instead. On the 21st
No 682 Sqn's 'A' Flight moved to Vasto, in Italy, where it joined the Desert
Air Force's No 285 Wing to take over demands for the Eighth Army.

# OPERATING ALONE

As the Allies prepared to invade Sicily, July saw No 680 Sqn continue
its lonely vigil over southern Greece and the islands of the Aegean. On
the 1st, 'B' Flight completed its move to Derna, in Libya, from where it

would be better placed to monitor Crete and the Greek mainland. August saw 'C' Flight's Flg Off Moss (BR416) conduct No 680 Sqn's first ever low-level mission on the 9th when he obtained oblique photographs of Rhodes. The following day the squadron received its first Spitfire PR XI with the delivery to Kilo 8 of EN661. On 21 August Sqn Ldr J G Cole flew it to Derna, from where he carried out No 680 Sqn's first operational PR XI sortie when he successfully photographed Piraeus and Melos.

September saw the last F VI/PR (BS106) withdrawn from the unit. Although not purpose-built for the role, the F VI/PR was the first PR Spitfire variant to feature a pressurised cockpit, but sadly its performance at height was a disappointment.

Throughout the summer No 680 Sqn's Cyprus detachment carried out a detailed survey of all of the major Dodecanese Islands in anticipation of an Italian surrender, at which point British forces intended to seize Rhodes and Kos. With the armistice of 8 September the Italian garrisons in the Dodecanese laid down their arms, but German troops already on Rhodes acted quickly and by the 11th had secured most of the island. Despite this, the British pressed on, and by the 18th had occupied a number of other islands, including Leros and Kos. These landings were only possible because of the photographs secured by No 680 Sqn's 'C' Flight, which continued to monitor the evolving situation with twice daily coverage of all major locations in the region.

At Tocra, in Libya, from where 'B' Flight was now operating, a watch on the airfields and ports of Crete and Greece showed a marked increase in shipping and air activity as the Germans rushed reinforcements to the Dodecanese. During the morning of 1 October Flg Off J G Huggins covered Piraeus and Athens, with his photographs showing the presence of a new type of German landing craft. The vessel was in the process of being built, and it appeared to be made of prefabricated parts. Two days later, the enemy launched a combined airborne and amphibious assault on Kos, and by the 4th the British garrison had been forced to surrender.

The failure to determine German intentions in a timely manner was largely caused by the geographically dispersed area over which No 680 Sqn's various flights were operating. The distances involved caused delays in responding to requests and processing information.

On 10 November 'C' Flight's Flg Off D O'Leary successfully covered Amorgos and Stampalia. When his photographs were examined, they showed 14 vessels leaving Stampalia, which interpreters determined were part of an invasion force intended for Leros and included prefabricated landing craft of the type first seen at Piraeus in October. On the 12th news was received that the Germans had indeed invaded Leros. For the remainder of the month 'C' Flight continued to monitor enemy activity in the region, but by the 17th Leros was under German control. With their position in the Dodecanese untenable, British troops were evacuated and by the end of the month the Germans had occupied all of the islands.

As 1943 drew to a close No 680 Sqn found itself still mainly equipped with Spitfire PR IVs, although these were now being supplemented by increasing numbers of PR XIs. In the Dodecanese campaign the PR organisation was faced with an enormous task in trying to cover a huge geographical area like the Aegean, but the squadron had risen to the challenge and rarely failed to provide the desired coverage.

# COMMAND CHANGE

By the start of 1944 the Allied armies in Italy were approaching the main German defensive position – Winter/Gustav Line – south of Rome. A major reorganisation of Allied air forces in the Mediterranean had taken place during the previous December when MAC and the Northwest African Air Forces were amalgamated to form the Mediterranean Allied Air Forces (MAAF). This was soon followed by a corresponding change in the PR organisation when, on 1 January 1944, the NAPRW was re-designated the Mediterranean Allied Photographic Reconnaissance Command (MAPRC). However, it continued to control all US and British strategic PR, assets including No 336(PR) Wing at San Severo.

Whilst the Spitfire squadrons of the latter unit were still heavily committed to providing tactical PR for the Allied armies in Italy, the nature of their work was becoming increasingly connected with the strategic bombing campaign. On 16 February, No 682 Sqn was informed it was to provide two Spitfires per day to fulfil tactical demands for the US Fifth Army, thus relieving No 683 Sqn of the duty. Two days later, No 682 Sqn's 'A' Flight returned to San Severo from Vasto, its place and commitments to the Eighth Army taken over by a detachment from No 683 Sqn.

By the start of March Mediterranean strategic bombing attacks were fully coordinated with those from Britain. The MAPRC became responsible for an area covering southern Germany, Austria, Czechoslovakia, Hungary, Bulgaria and Romania. March also saw a concerted interdiction campaign against the transportation network in northern and central Italy in an effort to prevent supplies reaching the German frontline. Much of the pre- and post-strike reconnaissance for the attacks would be the responsibility of Nos 682 and 683 Sqns. During April increased numbers of railway marshalling yards were added to the target lists in connection with a bombing campaign to interdict German supply lines, although both squadrons still maintained their commitments to tactical targets along the frontline.

On 13 April, Sqn Ldr J Morgan photographed factories and airfields around Vienna before covering the results of bombing attacks on Zagreb and Split during the return flight. This sortie was outside the range of operations normally allocated to No 682 Sqn, but its success meant Vienna would soon become a routine target for Spitfires. A small detachment was formed by the squadron towards the end of the month when Spitfire PR XI PA867 proceeded to Alghero, on Sardinia, on the 28th for coverage of the south coast of France to meet US Army demands. Flg Off D Redman flew the detachment's first sortie on the 29th when he successfully covered beaches and ports between Port-la-Nouvelle and Sète.

April had also seen MAPRC re-designated the Mediterranean Allied Photographic Reconnaissance Wing (MAPRW), but it made no difference to the organisational structure.

During May the Allied armies in Italy finally succeeded in breaking the Gustav line. The reconnaissance tasks carried out that month by Nos 682 and 683 Sqns remained varied, with both units continuing to undertake tactical operations. The aircraft based at San Severo now covered an ever expanding area in support of strategic bombing attacks. On the 19th No 683 Sqn flew a record eight sorties from San Severo. These included one mission flown

Spitfire PR XI EN671 'G' was assigned to the No 682 Sqn detachment at Pomigliano in June 1944. Four months earlier, the squadron had taken over the requirement to fulfil tactical demands for the US Fifth Army. Flying from forward bases, the detachment provided long focal length coverage for the Americans. For the first 19 days of August 1944 EN671 was the only serviceable aircraft of the detachment, flying 24 sorties during the period. The Spitfire was lost on 28 December 1944 whilst serving with No 683 Sqn (*Author's Collection*)

by Plt Off A D Lackey to the Vienna area. During the course of the mission he became the first No 683 Sqn pilot to fly over Czechoslovak territory.

On 1 June Plt Off J R McLaughlin made 19 runs over a new defensive line that was being constructed along the northern Apennines. The new position was the Gothic Line, which would stop the Allied advance for many months to come.

During this period the tactical detachments were on the move to keep up with the Allied advance. For the No 683 Sqn detachment, the first of four moves occurred on 6 June when it relocated to Aquino, No 285 Wing having been switched to the west coast to support the elements of the Eighth Army operating on that sector of the front, before finally ending up at Orvieto/Main on the 24th. Two days earlier, No 682 Sqn's Flt Sgt G Jack had been tasked with an urgent D/A request for industrial targets around Munich. This was the first visit to the Bavarian city by a Spitfire based in Italy, the area normally being covered by Mosquitos.

On 3 July Plt Off S P Johnson (PA905) attempted to cover the Danube after recent mining operations, but when over Yugoslavia his PR XI developed a serious oil leak and he had to make for home. He was able to land at San Severo, and as he taxied to dispersal his engine seized – Johnson had had a very lucky escape after flying more than 400 miles with a defective engine.

By the middle of the month Allied forces had made steady progress north, forcing the Germans to fall back to the Gothic Line. The No 682 Sqn detachment supporting the US Fifth Army transferred forward to Follonica on the 15th. It was well used to the frequent moves, which had little impact on operations. The squadron's Sardinia detachment was also on the move, relocating to Borgo, on Corsica, on the 16th in order to be nearer to the French coast.

There was quite a stir at San Severo on 15 August with the news that a No 60 Sqn SAAF Mosquito had been engaged over Leipheim by a Me 262. Due to increased reports of jet activity over southern Germany, more sorties to this area were assigned to Spitfires when the Mosquito proved too vulnerable to attack.

15 August also saw the US Seventh Army commence Operation *Dragoon* with landings in southeastern France. On the day of the invasion, three

sorties were carried out from Borgo. One of them was a 3 hr 10 min mission flown by Flg Off P H Taggart to the Rhône Valley, where he covered 11 bridges. August also saw a number of sorties flown to Munich by Spitfires, but none reported any jet activity. This changed on the 23rd when Flt Lt H C V Hawker (PA936) had No 683 Sqn's first encounter with jets;

'I was west of Munich after having covered four airfields. Out of habit, I looked behind and to my horror I saw an aircraft about 100 ft away at my level. It looked like it must have approached me from the stern before turning away, but I was not aware of being fired upon. I noticed a second aircraft to port and slightly astern. I made a sharp climbing turn over the enemy aircraft, which shot past me. It reappeared about 1000 yards off my starboard side and then tried to get behind me. When it was about 600 yards astern I made a very steep climbing turn to port and it overshot and appeared to give up the chase.'

This encounter occurred only 20 miles east of Lechfeld, from where it was known that the Me 262s of *Erprobungskommando* 262 were operating. Hawker estimated that the enemy aircraft were at least 100 mph faster than his own. The following day, No 683 Sqn's Flt Lt F N Crane was briefed to cover targets south of Munich. He took off from San Severo at 0843 hrs in PR XI EN338, but nothing further was heard of him. It seems highly likely that he fell victim to Oberfeldwebel Heinz-Helmut Baudach of *Erprobungskommando* 262, who claimed a Spitfire northwest of Innsbruck. It had long been the boast of the PRUs that their Spitfires could outrun and outclimb anything in the sky at high altitude, but the appearance of the Me 262 radically altered that situation.

September saw American and Free French forces in southern France continue with their rapid advance. On 1 September No 682 Sqn's Corsica detachment, now known as the 'B' Detachment, transferred to Le Luc, in southern France. After a series of moves the detachment ended the month at Dijon-Longvic, from where most of the sorties flown were to targets along the Franco-German frontier.

Careful planning and detailed intelligence had made *Dragoon* a great success, with the PR Spitfires playing a significant role in the operation. By the end of September the newly named French First Army and the US Seventh Army became the US 6th Army Group, and No 682 Sqn's 'B' Detachment continued to provide PR in support of the command.

In Italy both Spitfire detachments were kept very busy with frequent demands for coverage of the frontline and enemy rear areas. As was now usual, both units made a number of moves during the month, with No 683 Sqn's detachment ending up at Rimini and No 682 Sqn's 'A' Detachment at Florence/Peretola.

The threat posed by German jets caused No 106(PR) Group in Britain to request that MAPRW take over all routine cover for targets in southern Germany around the Munich area. High Mosquito losses had led to a prohibition on the type operating where the Me 262 was known to be active, and Spitfires flying from Britain to southern Bavaria were at the edge of their range even with the largest drop tanks. MAPRW Spitfires, however, could reach the area on internal fuel.

The situation improved marginally on 6 September when two PR XIXs arrived from Britain, one being allocated to No 682 Sqn and the other to

No 683 Sqn. The latter's first PR XIX sortie was carried out on the 10th when Flt Sgt H M Rittman (RM626) attempted to cover airfields near Munich, but he found the whole area obscured by cloud. Two days later No 682 Sqn had more success when Plt Off R W E Hickes (RM640) covered the results of bombing attacks against jet bases at Lechfeld and Leipheim.

At the start of September the Commander in Chief MAAF, Lt Gen I C Eaker, initiated a study into the feasibility of making US photographic units in the Mediterranean independent of the MAPRW, which resulted in the latter's disbandment on 1 October 1944. However, No 682 Sqn's 'A' and 'B' Detachments continued to provide tactical cover for US forces in Italy and southern France, and No 336(PR) Wing strived to fulfil all British PR demands. By October MAAF reported that the commitment to use only Mediterranean-based reconnaissance aircraft over southern Germany was causing many abortive sorties and casualties due to interception by jet aircraft. This fact, coupled with increased demands for cover of targets in Austria and western Hungary, combined to keep No 336(PR) Wing's San Severo-based Spitfires busy.

On the 8th, No 682 Sqn's Flg Off R J H Strantzen took off in PR XIX RM639 to cover rail targets between Budapest and Vienna but failed to return. His Spitfire was the first PR XIX to be lost in the Mediterranean theatre. During November No 682 Sqn's 'B' Detachment continued to provide support for the 6th Army Group, and it was on the move again on the 5th when it transferred to Nancy. The month saw the detachment take over formal responsibility for covering the southwestern corner of Germany from the units based in Italy. It also brought a reorganisation in operational areas for No 336(PR) Wing's Spitfire units whereby No 683 Sqn's longer range trips would now concentrate on targets around Vienna, whilst No 682 Sqn would deal with most of the demands around Munich.

On the 27th Plt Off L Courtney failed to return from a mission to southern Germany. He was flying RM626, which became the first No 683 Sqn PR XIX to be lost. The squadron's detached flight transferred to Forli on 4 December. In what was a relatively rare occurrence for the detachment, Flt Lt F W W Haward (MB776) was intercepted on a mission to cover targets in the Padova-Vicenza area on the 29th;

'The aircraft made a fast turn to port and passed under me. It was much faster than my PR XI and managed to get on my tail. Even with my aircraft at full speed it was gaining, but when it got to within 400 yards I made a violent turn. It then rapidly climbed into the sun and I lost sight of it.'

Although Haward did get a good view of the aircraft, he was certain it was not a Me 262 but did think it was jet-propelled.

With 1944 at an end, the German lines in Italy remained unbroken and Allied commanders were left with little choice but to call off their offensive until better spring weather enabled them to resume the attack. None of this made any difference to the Spitfire PRUs, which continued to fly whenever possible for the photographs they brought back were always highly sought after.

## BACKWATER

With the British failure in the Dodecanese during 1943, the eastern Mediterranean became a backwater for the remainder of the war.

The bulk of No 680 Sqn's work at the start of 1944 continued to be connected with tracking shipping movements in the Aegean. The unit was gradually receiving more Spitfire PR XIs, while its old PR IVs were slowly removed from the inventory. Most were passed on to No 74 OTU for training.

February 1944 saw the squadron receive its first two Mosquitos, as it had finally been decided by MAAF that No 680 Sqn would be the unit to re-equip with the type. By May 'B' Flight was equipped with equal numbers of Spitfires and Mosquitos, although it was the former that carried out the majority of sorties due to serviceability issues with the de Havilland aircraft. For 'C' Flight the level of operations would have been greater but for the shortage of aircraft caused by the decision to withdraw the PR IV from service – the last operational sortie undertaken by the variant with No 680 Sqn was carried out by Flt Lt G Bellerby (EN155) on the 12th when he successfully covered Rhodes and Kos.

During August MAAF announced its intention that No 680 Sqn would be solely equipped with the Mosquito, but ongoing serviceability problems with the type made it necessary to retain six Spitfire PR XIs on strength. This change caused the squadron to undergo a major reorganisation, with 'C' Flight being recalled to Egypt, where it took over the unit's non-operational duties from 'A' Flight. Consequently, 'A' Flight assumed operational duties equipped with Mosquitos, and by the end of the month began moving to Italy to operate under No 336(PR) Wing control. On 11 August 'B' Flight at Tocra assumed responsibility for

No 682 Sqn's Flt Lt Hank Oldfield (left) and Flg Off Jimmy Rawson enjoy the 'balmy' Mediterranean weather at San Severo in January 1945. The Spitfire PR XIX they are standing in front of is fitted with a slipper-style drop tank. Both Nos 682 and 683 Sqns of No 336(PR) Wing operated the PR XIX, but neither unit ever had more than a handful on strength, and all were unpressurised versions of the type (*Author's Collection*)

covering the Dodecanese, this being in addition to its usual commitments over Crete and Greece.

By October Soviet advances in southeastern Europe threatened to cut off German troops in Greece, forcing them to begin withdrawing from the mainland but leaving garrisons in place on Crete and the Dodecanese. This led to a further reorganisation of No 680 Sqn in November. 'B' Flight continued to operate from Tocra for the first half of the month, at which point it returned to Kilo 8/Matariyah on the 15th. It was planned that all work in the eastern Mediterranean would now be carried out from Egypt. On its return, 'B' Flight surrendered its last remaining Spitfire PR XIs and became solely equipped with Mosquitos.

Earlier that same month a new 'C' Flight had been formed at Matariyah, and it took over all remaining Spitfire PR XI operations and the greater share of the remaining work over the German-occupied islands of the Aegean. For much of December 'C' Flight's Spitfires carried out routine operations, although the deteriorating security situation in Greece resulted in a number of special commitments in the Athens area where an insurgency by communist guerrillas had broken out. On the 28th Flg Off D B Brown flew PA845 to Hassani, in Athens, from where he carried out the first low-level missions to photograph insurgent positions the following day. The detachment at Hassani continued for the first two weeks of January 1945, during which period Flg Off Brown and Flt Lt J P Kelley carried out 18 sorties, all of which obtained a wealth of photographic intelligence.

At the start of February, 'B' and 'C' Flights were amalgamated to form a new composite 'B' Flight equipped with both Spitfires and Mosquitos. On the 25th, No 680 Sqn moved to Deversoir, in the Canal Zone, from

where 'B' Flight's Spitfires carried out most of the operational flying for the remainder of the war. The unconditional surrender of all remaining German forces on 8 May saw the squadron still covering Aegean targets. When news of the cessation of hostilities came through, Flt Lt C V S Stevens (PA845) was already airborne on a mission to Rhodes. This final effort brought the squadron's war to an end, by which point it had completed more than 5000 operational sorties, the majority of them in PR Spitfires. The unit would continue to operate Spitfire PR XIs until July 1946, but in September No 680 Sqn was re-designated No 13 Sqn, thus bringing to an end the history of the RAF's second oldest wartime PRU.

In Italy at the end of 1944, heavy winter rains had halted the Allied offensive. With lessened activity along the front, 1945 saw the PR detachments supporting the Allied armies switching their attention to German communications in the rear area, whilst from San Severo both Nos 682 and 683 Sqns continued their strategic tasks deeper into enemy territory. March saw an intensification of attacks by Allied tactical aircraft on transportation targets in Italy. No 682 Sqn's 'A' Detachment completed a total of 47 sorties for the US Fifth Army during the month. Likewise, No 683 Sqn's Forli detachment flew at every opportunity to fulfil demands for the Eighth Army.

Along the Western Front Allied armies made renewed efforts to clear the last German positions west of the Rhine. For No 682 Sqn's 'B' Detachment at Nancy, most of the requests for 36-inch photographic cover came from the French, who needed imagery along the Rhine. On 25 March the unit was informed that its attachment to the US 6th Army Group was complete.

In April No 336(PR) Wing's operational area continued to shrink. The diminishing number of sorties flown from San Severo during the course of the month was a reflection of the reduced demand for photography. On the 15th, No 682 Sqn's WO R S Baker (RM630) attempted to cover targets in the Munich area but found all of his objectives obscured by cloud. RM630 was the only PR XIX remaining on strength with the unit, and Baker's sortie proved to be the last operational mission by the type with the squadron.

At the beginning of April, the Allies had commenced their spring offensive in Italy, and after initial resistance was overcome both the British Eighth and the US Fifth armies broke through German frontlines. The two aircraft of No 682 Sqn's 'A' Detachment flew continually during the month, but on the 30th the Americans issued formal notification that the detachment was no longer required and was to return to San Severo. On 2 May German forces in Italy and western Austria surrendered unconditionally. This did not, however, include those troops east of the Isondo River. Consequently, cover of the Istrian Peninsula and northwestern Yugoslavia was still required, although the level of demand slackened significantly.

On 6 May, No 682 Sqn's last operational sortie was flown by Flg Off J Rawson in Spitfire PR XI PL980 when he obtained partial coverage of Zagreb. The following day No 683 Sqn's detachment made its last wartime move when it transferred to Treviso. From here, it flew the unit's final sortie of the war on 8 May when Plt Off H Peebles (PA909) covered the railway between Trieste and Gorizia. That day the formal cessation of hostilities in

Europe was announced. No 682 Sqn remained at San Severo, where it was ultimately disbanded in September 1945. Originally formed as No 4 PRU in 1942, the unit had had its baptism of fire during the fighting in Vichy French North Africa, and from that point forward its Spitfires provided constant photographic cover.

No 683 Sqn's main body also remained at San Severo in May, and although the unit would not be formally disbanded until 21 December 1945, by the end of September it had effectively ceased to be a regular flying unit. Like its sister Spitfire PRU, No 683 Sqn had come into existence in 1942 during a very difficult period for the Allies in the Mediterranean. As the Spitfire Flight of No 69 Sqn, it had carried out the vital PR function from Malta at a time when few other aircraft could operate from the island. During its existence the unit had flown nearly 4500 operational sorties.

# FAR EAST PR OPERATIONS

At the start of the war strategic PR in India and the Far East was merely an afterthought. By May 1942, the Japanese had advanced through Burma to the Indian frontier, where the onset of the monsoon forced them to pause. During that month, a new No 3 PRU was formed with one flight of B-25s and another equipped with Hurricanes. In September, AOC-in-C India, Air Marshal Sir Richard Peirse, appealed for PR Spitfires to enable his command to undertake the support work necessary for both defensive and offensive operations.

On 24 September, Wg Cdr Wise and Sgt W H L Cusack proceeded to the Middle East to collect the first two machines. They arrived back at Dum Dum, near Calcutta, on 10 October, Wise at the controls of BP911 and Cusack in BP935. Both aircraft were PR IVs camouflaged in the overall Royal Blue scheme used by No 2 PRU. On the 19th Wise (BP911) carried out his unit's first Spitfire sortie when he covered sections

Spitfire PR IV BP911, with Wg Cdr Stewart Wise at the controls, arrives at Dum Dum on 10 October 1942. Following an appeal by AOC-in-C India, Air Marshal Sir Richard Peirse, for modern PR aircraft in-theatre, two Spitfires were allocated to No 3 PRU in India, both machines having previously flown with No 2 PRU. Wg Cdr Wise carried out his unit's first operational PR Spitfire sortie, and the first ever by a Spitfire of any type in Southeast Asia, on 19 October when he attempted to photograph enemy airfields in the Shwebo, Mandalay, Maymo and Monywa areas of Burma. Thick cloud cover prevented him from photographing his primary objectives, however, and he had to content himself with covering short sections of the Chindwin River (*Author's Collection*)

of the Chindwin River. During January 1943, No 3 PRU was informed that in line with plans to reorganise overseas PR assets, the unit would be re-designated No 681 Sqn.

Southeast Asia was the last theatre of the war to see the use of PR Spitfires. By January 1943 the newly renamed No 681 Sqn was still mainly equipped with PR Hurricanes, but increasing use was being made of the few Spitfires on strength. On the 25th – the same day No 681 Sqn was formed from No 3 PRU – WO F D C Brown (PR IV BR431) flew the new unit's first Spitfire sortie when he successfully photographed targets in central Burma.

By March PR operations were starting to expand in size and scope. In Southeast Asia, the Allies were forced to assemble information on Japanese intentions largely from scratch, relying heavily on PR. On the 25th two successful Spitfire sorties were flown. As was now becoming standard practice, both aircraft landed at Dohazari on their return to refuel. As the pilots prepared to fly back to Dum Dum, Dohazari was attacked by Japanese bombers. Although BR418 received shrapnel damage, its pilot, Flt Lt M W Coombes, escaped injury. Flg Off F D Procter was not so lucky, receiving serious wounds to his arm. His aircraft, BP911, was so badly damaged in the bombing that it was beyond economical repair and duly became the first Spitfire to be lost due to enemy action in Southeast Asia.

The poor weather conditions with which pilots were often confronted were demonstrated on 8 June. After successfully covering most of his objectives, WO Brown (AB318) set course for Chittagong, but cloud over the Chin Hills prevented him from landing at the forward base. He altered course directly for Dum Dum, and as he flew further west he encountered an extensive frontal system;

'I hit a series of violent up-draughts which put me in a spin, but as I tried to correct it my head was forced down between my knees and I passed out. When I came to, I was falling through the air and could see large pieces of my aircraft plummeting to earth.'

Pulling the ripcord of his parachute, he landed safely on the ground. Brown was then taken to hospital to recover from injuries sustained in the incident.

The monsoon weather continued to disrupt flying, but there was some good news as more pilots and PR IVs continued to arrive directly from Britain. Unlike the machines that had come from the Middle

By the time this photograph of Spitfire PR IV BP911 was taken, it had been assigned to No 681 Sqn at Dum Dum. On 25 March 1943 Flg Off Freddie Procter successfully covered Toungoo, Tennant, Kalawya and Oktwin in the aircraft before landing at Dohazari to refuel. After topping up his tanks, Procter taxied BP911 in preparation to return to Dum Dum, but as he did so Dohazari was attacked by enemy bombers. BP911 was badly damaged by exploding ordnance and Procter seriously wounded. Whilst the latter eventually recovered and returned to operations, BP911 was too badly damaged to be repaired and was scrapped (*Author's Collection*)

No 681 Sqn's WO Francis Brown poses with the ripcord from his parachute after bailing out of PR IV AB318 on 8 June 1943. In Southeast Asia it was often the conditions that were a bigger threat than the Japanese. Having successfully covered targets in central Burma, Brown encountered rapidly deteriorating weather conditions as he headed for Chittagong. Changing course directly for Dum Dum, he was forced to fly through an extensive frontal system. After fighting to maintain control of AB318 for 20 minutes, his aircraft entered a spin and Brown passed out. When he came to, he was plummeting to earth with parts of his Spitfire falling all around him. Once safely on the ground, he was hospitalised with severe subconjunctival haemorrhaging in both eyes. Upon being released from hospital, Brown returned to No 681 Sqn but soon after was found to have fractured his back and was repatriated to New Zealand (*Author's Collection*)

East, those from Britain were camouflaged in standard PRU Blue.

At the start of August authority was given to increase the establishment of No 681 Sqn to 20 Spitfires, and to form a new PRU that would ultimately be equipped with Mosquitos. On 6 October the first Spitfire PR XI (MB889) was delivered to the squadron, followed a week later by the formation of the second PRU, No 684 Sqn, leaving No 681 Sqn equipped with Spitfires and Hurricanes. On the 18th Plt Off A R Lehman carried out No 681 Sqn's first operation in a Spitfire PR XI when he successfully covered special areas in the Kale Valley. It was intended that No 684 Sqn would undertake longer-ranged work, leaving No 681 Sqn's Spitfires to perform all other tasks.

The expansion of RAF PR assets coincided with a major reorganisation of all Allied air forces in the region. To coordinate the work of British and American units in Bengal and Assam, the Eastern Air Command (EAC) was formed, under which No 171(PR) Wing would soon be activated to control the operations of Nos 681 and 684 Sqns.

Despite the advances made by the PR organisation in 1943, very little long-range work had been undertaken to date. This steadily changed as No 681 Sqn's Spitfires increasingly flew deeper and deeper into Burma, with flights as far south as Rangoon now starting to become routine.

During 1944, it was intended to launch a series of offensives in Burma from the west whilst American-supported Chinese forces attacked from the northeast. No 681 Sqn was heavily involved, providing cover for all of these operations. In February the squadron became part of the Photographic Reconnaissance Force (PRF) that was formed to coordinate British and American PR efforts.

On 5 March, Flt Lt C B P Davies (BP880) failed to return from a sortie to southern Burma. This was the last operational PR IV loss suffered by the unit during the war. Three days later, elements of the Japanese Fifteenth Army began crossing the Chindwin with the aim of capturing Imphal and Kohima. During this period considerable effort was expended by No 681 Sqn in covering Japanese airfields throughout Burma. It showed that the bulk of the enemy's air assets in the country were being concentrated for operations along the Indian frontier. On 23 March, the squadron suffered another loss when Flg Off V E Cross failed to return from a sortie to cover airfields in central Burma. His aircraft (PA853) was the first PR XI to be lost by the squadron.

On 5 May, No 681 Sqn moved to Alipore, and it began operating from the new location the same day. During May many of the unit's weary

PR IVs were replaced with PR XIs, although the older aircraft continued to see regular use. The following month the squadron became the last PRU in the RAF to still be using the Spitfire PR IV operationally. The lack of regular fighter opposition meant PR IVs could operate safely and achieve excellent results long after they had been relegated to a training role elsewhere.

On 6 August, No 681 Sqn detached a section of Spitfires to operate from Comilla in direct support of HQ 3rd TAF. The establishment of the Comilla detachment coincided with an advance to clear the Japanese from west of the Chindwin River. During November a large number of missions were flown by the squadron to support operations by the British Army to establish bridgeheads over the Chindwin and for a resumption of the advance along the Arakan coast. On the 30th, Flg Off C I Younger carried out the last operational sortie undertaken by the unit in a PR IV (BR661) when he successfully photographed roads in central Burma. Spitfire PR IVs had served with the unit since October 1942, when No 3 PRU became the first unit in Southeast Asia to operate Spitfires.

On 3 January 1945 Akyab Island was invaded, with last-minute coverage having been provided by two No 681 Sqn Spitfires on the 1st. Flg Off R Lauchland took large-scale vertical images from 6000 ft using moving-film F63 cameras, whilst WO W J H Wells carried out low-level oblique runs along the coast.

By late January Allied progress in central Burma and along the Arakan coast offered the opportunity of liberating Rangoon before the monsoon season halted offensive operations. No 681 Sqn's efforts were considerable during January, with 187 sorties flown. This high tempo of operations was maintained during the spring. Most sorties were to central and southern Burma, with many missions flown to the area between the Irrawaddy and Sittang rivers, as well as to Rangoon. Thanks to extensive coverage of the latter area by No 681 Sqn, Allied forces were able to occupy the city on 2 May when it became apparent that the Japanese had evacuated.

WO Norman Haye of No 681 Sqn takes off from Chittagong in Spitfire PR XI PA934 'T' on 7 December 1944, bound for the Burmese town of Pyokkwe. In a sortie lasting 2 hr 40 min, he successfully photographed the railway line between Pyokkwe and Mandalay, before landing back at Chittagong to refuel and then returning to Alipore. No 681 Sqn did not receive its first PR XI until 6 October 1943, and continued to use PR IVs operationally until November 1944 (*Author's Collection*)

Spitfire PR XI PL969 'P' of No 681 Sqn's Forward Detachment was photographed parked in front of a Hurricane IIC at Monywa. By February 1945, the British Fourteenth Army had reached the Irrawaddy River on a broad front and established a number of bridgeheads on the far bank. During the month the Forward Detachment moved to Monywa, although the airfield had been in use as a refuelling base by the squadron's Spitfires for a number of days. The first sortie originating from Monywa was flown by WO K J Collins on 17 February when he obtained obliques of Yenangyaug and Taungwingya in PR XI PL960 (*Author's Collection*)

For much of May the main body of No 681 Sqn had flown from Alipore, but on the 20th it began moving to Mingaladon, north of Rangoon, from where it flew its first operational sortie on the 25th. On 1 June No 347(PR) Wing was formed to control the RAF element of the PRF, which was about to be disbanded due to American forces ending operations in Burma. No 347(PR) Wing would control the operations of Nos 681 and 684 Sqns for the remainder of the war.

On 19 June, WO M H Harris (PR XI PL849) disappeared on a sortie to Tavoy, this proving to be the last Spitfire lost on operations by No 681 Sqn. Towards the end of the following month, the squadron received its first examples of the Spitfire PR XIX, the type making its operational debut in-theatre on 28 July when Wg Cdr D B Pearson (PS918) covered the airfield at Tak, in Siam.

At the end of the month another unit in Southeast Asia received PR Spitfires. No 28 Sqn was a Tac/R unit equipped with Hurricanes, but by July it only had a handful of serviceable machines left. On the 30th the squadron was informed that Spitfire PR XIs were to be allocated from No 681 Sqn, with the first example received the following day. On 5 August a pair of PR XIs flown by Flt Lts S J Smith and F A Dawson flew No 28 Sqn's first operational Spitfire sorties when they carried out a successful Tac/R of Thaton and Bilin.

By August, No 681 Sqn had five PR XIXs on strength, but because of serviceability issues they were generally only used on short sorties. On the 9th Wg Cdr Pearson (PS918) carried out numerous runs along the Sittang River from 10,000 ft, the sortie only lasting a little over an hour. This also proved to be No 681 Sqn's last operational PR XIX mission of the war. That day the Americans had used their second atomic bomb on Nagasaki. The employment of these weapons forced the Japanese to surrender on 15 August, bringing World War 2 to an end.

The very last wartime sorties flown by PR Spitfires were, ironically, made by newly converted No 28 Sqn. On the 15th Flt Lts M R Alston and F Smith successfully covered Mokpalin and Thaton during the morning before the official announcement of the Japanese surrender was made. No 28 Sqn was

ordered to hand its PR XIs back to No 681 Sqn on the 22nd, after which it reverted to using Hurricanes. For No 681 Sqn, the end of the war meant the unit would now be employed on survey work in countries previously occupied by the Japanese. Throughout this time it continued to fly Spitfire PR XIs and PR XIXs until, on 1 August 1946, it was renumbered No 34 Sqn.

Of all theatres to which PR Spitfires were committed during World War 2, their operations in Southeast Asia probably assumed greater significance than any other. Often aerial photographs were the only means by which the activities of the Japanese in Burma could be monitored. The Spitfires of No 681 Sqn duly supplied much of the intelligence on which Allied forces relied.

The defeat of the Japanese brought World War 2 to an end. More than any conflict to date, it had seen intelligence gathering play a vital role. For the Allies, it was estimated that as much as 80 per cent of all intelligence was gained from aerial photography, much of it derived from the cameras installed in Spitfires. The exacting nature of the work, and the performance required to fulfil it, meant there were few aircraft and even fewer pilots capable of rising to the challenge. PR using high-speed, high-altitude aircraft had started as an experiment pursued by a free-thinking maverick with the backing of a few far-sighted leaders, but once the principle was established PR became a vital component of every Allied campaign, with the intelligence gained considered necessary for the planning of any operation.

PR Spitfires ultimately saw service against the three principal partners of the Axis alliance in World War 2. Even though supplemented by the Mosquito from 1941, the Spitfire remained one of the RAF's primary strategic reconnaissance platforms. Its capabilities even led to the USAAF adopting the type for some of its own reconnaissance needs. Much of the work carried out was mundane and repetitive, but PR Spitfires were also responsible for some of the most significant intelligence finds of the war. PR allowed Allied leaders to monitor almost every aspect of the enemy's activity, and act accordingly, and it is a tribute to the Spitfire that it was the only aircraft capable of fulfilling this role throughout the whole conflict.

PR XIX PM512 'N' of No 681 Sqn sits at Seletar with other PR Spitfires immediately post-war. The last unit to fly the PR XIX operationally was Burma-based No 681 Sqn, which had only received its first examples of the aircraft in late July 1945. Due to serviceability issues with its new aircraft, No 681 Sqn flew few missions with the PR XIX – those flown were generally restricted to short range. Following the Japanese surrender, No 681 Sqn continued to be equipped with the PR XI and PR XIX, and it carried out extensive survey work over Southeast Asia before being disbanded on 1 August 1946 (*Author's Collection*)

# APPENDICES

## COLOUR PLATES COMMENTARY

### 1

**Spitfire I PR Type A N3071 of the Special Survey Flight, Nancy, France, December 1939**

N3071 was one of the first two Spitfires delivered to the Heston Flight in October 1939. Fitted with an F24 camera in each wing, it was N3071 flown by Flt Lt 'Shorty' Longbottom that conducted the first PR Spitfire sortie of the war, on 20 November, when he attempted to cover targets in the Aachen area. N3071 was lost on 21 April 1940 when No 212 Sqn's Flg Off Cecil Milne was intercepted over southern Germany by Bf 109s.

### 2

**Spitfire I PR Type B P9331 '9' of No 212 Sqn, Meaux/ Villenoy, France, June 1940**

P9331 flew its first operational sortie on 8 May 1940 when Flt Lt Louis Wilson was tasked with covering the Rhine from the Dutch Frontier to Dusseldorf. The same pilot flew P9331 on 7 June when he successfully photographed German supply routes across Belgium. Later in the day Flg Off Allan Blackwell took off in the aircraft to complete the task, only to be forced to make an emergency landing at Rheims/Champagne with engine problems. P9331 was still sat there when the airfield was captured by German troops.

### 3

**Spitfire I PR Type C P9550 'LY 19' of 'A' Flight PDU, Wick, Scotland, early July 1940**

The Type C was the first variant to carry a vertical camera with a long focal length lens in the rear fuselage. In the 14 months that P9550 served with the PRU it flew more than 100 operational sorties, the last of which took place on 7 August 1941 when Flg Off Donald Steventon successfully covered Kiel. He was forced to fly through a storm front on his return, during which the aircraft entered a violent spin. Eventually recovering control at 7000 ft, Steventon returned to base, where the aircraft was found to have buckled mainplanes.

### 4

**Spitfire I PR Type D P9551 'LY' of 'A' Flight No 1 PRU, Ta Kali, Malta, January 1941**

P9551 was the first of two prototype Type D Spitfires, this variant having specially fabricated wing leading-edge fuel tanks. This aircraft made its operational debut on 29 October 1940, when the PRU's Flg Off Sam Millen attempted to cover Berlin. Finding his primary objectives obscured by cloud, he covered ports along Germany's Baltic and North Sea coasts, setting a new duration record of 5 hr 30 min in the process. On 19 January 1941 Flt Lt Peter Corbishley attempted to photograph Genoa and La Spezia in P9551, but exceptionally strong tail winds forced him to land on Malta. It was not until 2 February that conditions allowed the pilot to attempt to complete his task, only for his aircraft to be hit by flak over Leghorn, forcing Corsbishley to bail out. At the time of its loss P9551 was the only Type D in service with No 1 PRU.

### 5

**Spitfire I PR Type F X4712 'LY' of 'A' Flight No 3 PRU, Alconbury, Cambridgeshire, March 1941**

No 3 PRU was formed to fulfil the targeting and damage assessment requirements of RAF Bomber Command. Reaching the unit on 9 January 1941, X4712 was the first Type F assigned to No 3 PRU. It was flown operationally later that same day when Flg Off John Blount covered the German North Sea ports from 28,000 ft. On 9 April, Blount, again in X4712, failed to return from a mission to Bremen and Bremerhaven after being intercepted by Bf 109s.

### 6

**Spitfire I PR Type G (serial unknown) 'ZW-J' of No 140 Sqn, Benson, South Oxfordshire, September 1941**

The Type G was intended for low-level operations when cloud conditions precluded high-altitude photography. It was equipped with two vertical F24 cameras in the rear fuselage and an oblique F24 camera that could be configured to face either port or starboard. The cameras' combination of lenses allowed for photography below medium and low cloud. A variety of pale camouflage schemes were experimented with to enable the Type G to blend into cloud. However, when in service with RAF Army Co-operation Command's No 140 Sqn, most Type Gs were painted in the standard day fighter temperate land scheme.

### 7

**Spitfire V PR Type D R7056 'LY' of 'D' Flight No 1 PRU, Benson, South Oxfordshire, November 1941**

R7056 was the last of the initial batch of production Type Ds which were based on the Spitfire I airframe. The first production Type D, R7035, was received by No 1 PRU on 8 July 1941, from which point onwards a steady flow of new machines were delivered to Benson. R7056 arrived on 28 August and was assigned to 'D' Flight. All subsequent Type Ds were based on the Mk V, the first of which being AA781.

### 8

**Spitfire I PR Type G (PR VII) X4944 'LY' of 'K' Flight No 1 PRU, Detling, Kent, May 1942**

A veteran of 70 operational sorties with No 1 PRU, X4944 was eventually relegated to a training role with 'K' Flight at Detling. By this time the Type G had been renamed the PR VII. Throughout its operational career X4944 was camouflaged in the PRU's very pale green/almost white scheme.

### 9

**Spitfire PR IV Trop AB312 of 'A' Flight No 2 PRU, LG 28/ Burgh-el-Arab, Egypt, July 1942**

The first PR Spitfires were not based permanently overseas until 1942. On 17 March No 2 PRU received three examples of the PR IV, including AB312. Unlike the machines operating over northwest Europe, the aircraft of No 2 PRU were camouflaged with the darker Royal Blue scheme that was better suited to the clearer conditions found at altitude over the eastern Mediterranean. No 2 PRU's PR IVs were fitted with the bulky Vokes filter to remove the fine sand that was ever present in North Africa.

# 10

## Spitfire PR IV AB132 '01' of the 3rd Aviation Squadron/118th Reconnaissance Aviation Regiment, Vaenga, USSR, January 1943

AB132 was one of the four PR IVs used by the No 1 PRU detachment based at Vaenga in support of Operation *Orator* during autumn 1942. With the end of *Orator*, the surviving machines were handed over to the Air Force of the Soviet Northern Fleet, where they were assigned to the 3rd Aviation Squadron/118th Reconnaissance Aviation Regiment. Two subsequent RAF PR detachments to Vaenga also handed over their PR IVs to the same unit, and although the Soviets never had more than three or four serviceable machines, they made a useful contribution to the war effort in the Arctic.

# 11

## Spitfire PR IV Trop BP932 of No 683 Sqn, Luqa, Malta, February 1943

The first overseas unit to receive PR Spitfires was No 69 Sqn on Malta, its first example arriving on 7 March 1942. On 8 February 1943 the Spitfire Flight of No 69 Sqn became No 683 Sqn. BP932 served with both units and, interestingly, was camouflaged in No 2 PRU's Royal Blue scheme, even though there is no record of the aircraft ever having served with that unit.

# 12

## Spitfire PR IV Trop BP911 'T' of No 681 Sqn, Dum Dum, India, 25 March 1943

BP911 and BP935 were the first two PR Spitfires to be received by No 3 PRU in Southeast Asia. Delivered to the unit on 10 October 1942, both machines had originally served with No 2 PRU in the Middle East. When No 3 PRU was re-designated No 681 Sqn on 25 January 1943, BP911 continued to serve with the new unit. On 25 March, however, it was damaged beyond economical repair during a Japanese bombing attack on Dohazari, thus becoming the first Spitfire lost to enemy action in Southeast Asia.

# 13

## Spitfire PR XI EN654 of No 16 Sqn, Hartford Bridge, Hampshire, December 1943

No 16 Sqn joined No 34 Wing at the end of June 1943 and began converting to Spitfire PR XIs in August in machines borrowed from No 140 Sqn. It was not until November that the squadron was allocated its own aircraft. EN654 was amongst the first PR Spitfires delivered to the unit, and the aircraft flew its first operational sortie on 20 December when Flg Off Guy Cribb covered Cherbourg and Bayeux from 30,000 ft.

# 14

## Spitfire PR XI EN671 'G' of No 682 Sqn, Pomigliano, Italy, March 1944

On 16 February 1944 Flg Off Les Colquhoun flew EN671 on No 682 Sqn's first sortie from Pomigliano for the US Fifth Army when he successfully covered targets between Formia and Cassino. The aircraft was lost on 28 December 1944 when No 683 Sqn's Flg Off John Gourley failed to return from his first operational PR sortie. Briefed to cover the Istrian Peninsula, he issued a distress call which was fixed at 15 miles north of Pola, but no trace of pilot or aircraft were ever found.

# 15

## Spitfire PR XI EN664 'Q' *BRENDA* of 'B' Flight No 541 Sqn, St Eval, Cornwall, May 1944

With the disbandment of No 543 Sqn on 18 October 1943, the commitment to cover the ports along the west coast of France from St Eval became the responsibility of No 541 Sqn's 'B' Flight. The first sortie undertaken by the flight was carried out the following day when Plt Off Harold Herbert attempted to cover Brest in PR XI EN664. Due to the diminished strategic importance of western France, the detachment was recalled back to Benson to rejoin the main body of No 541 Sqn on 20 July 1944, EN664 having served with 'B' Flight throughout its time at St Eval.

# 16

## Spitfire PR X MD193 of No 541 Sqn, Benson, South Oxfordshire, 4 June 1944

It was anticipated that the performance advantage enjoyed by the PR XI over German fighters would eventually be superseded. As it was, interceptions were increasingly occurring at altitudes above 40,000 ft. This led to the introduction of the PR X, the first purpose-built high-altitude PR Spitfire. Incorporating the pressurised cabin of the F VII, it allowed pilots to withstand greater altitudes for longer periods. Only 16 examples of the PR X were built, and all served with Nos 541 and 542 Sqns. MD193 was the first example to reach Benson, being delivered to No 541 Sqn on 8 May 1944.

# 17

## Spitfire PR XIX RM633 of No 541 Sqn, Benson, South Oxfordshire, June 1944

The last wartime variant of the PR Spitfire was the Griffon-powered PR XIX. It was intended to be fitted with a pressurised cockpit, but the first examples to enter service with Nos 541 and 542 Sqns at Benson were unpressurised. Easily capable of flying in excess of 45,000 ft, the PR XIX was very fast, enjoying a significant speed advantage over the PR XI. RM633 was the first PR XIX to be lost on operations when its engine failed over the Channel on 15 June 1944. Sqn Ldr J H Saffery bailed out and was eventually rescued by a passing MTB on its way to patrol off the Belgian coast.

# 18

## Spitfire PR XI PA944 of the 14th PRS/7th PG(R), Mount Farm, Oxfordshire, September 1944

PA944 was one of a number of PR XIs delivered to the Eighth Air Force to provide PR for USAAF units flying on operations from Britain. By the time PA944 was received by the 7th PG(R) in April 1944, all Spitfire PR missions were being undertaken by the group's 14th PRS. On 12 September, Lt John Blyth successfully covered objectives in the Hanau and Eisenach areas in this aircraft, but on arrival back at Mount Farm the undercarriage would not lower. After loitering in the area for an hour, he was forced to make a wheels-up landing. By putting PA944 down on the grass next to the runway, minimal damage was done to the aircraft and Blyth was completely unharmed.

# 19

## Spitfire PR XI PL969 'P' of the Forward Detachment No 681 Sqn, Monywa, Burma, February 1945

During 1945 the advance of the British Fourteenth Army in Burma meant that the No 681 Sqn detachment operating in support was regularly called upon to move to new bases in order to stay in close contact with its controlling HQ. From January 1945 the unit was known as the Forward Detachment, and during the month the spinners on its aircraft were painted orange as a recognition aid for Allied fighters. The Forward Detachment moved from Kalemyo to Monywa on 17 February, flying its first sortie from the new base that same day.

## 20
### Spitfire PR XI MB950 of the 14th PRS/7th PG(R), Mount Farm, Oxfordshire, February 1945

MB950 was amongst the first Spitfire PR XIs delivered to the USAAF at Mount Farm in November 1943. Received on the 13th, the aircraft flew its first mission on the 25th with Lt Malcolm Hughes of the 22nd PRS at the controls. MB950 continued to serve with the 7th PG(R), and was one of the survivors handed back to the RAF at the beginning of April 1945 when the 14th PRS began re-equipping with the F-5 in anticipation of transferring to the Pacific.

## 21
### Spitfire PR XI PM151 of No 400 Sqn, Petit Brogel (B90), Belgium, March 1945

The success of *Veritable* – the operation to clear German troops from the west bank of the Rhine – led to another series of base moves for many of 2nd TAF's units. During the afternoon of 7 March 1945, No 400 Sqn's 19 Spitfire PR XIs made the short transfer flight from Eindhoven (B78) to Petit Brogel (B90). Due to poor weather, it was the 9th before the first operations were flown, and of the four attempted all were unsuccessful due to cloud.

## 22
### Spitfire PR XIX PM512 'N' of No 681 Sqn, Seletar, Singapore, spring 1946

The last unit to receive the Spitfire PR XIX during wartime was No 681 Sqn in Burma, with the first example (PS918) being delivered during July 1945. The aircraft was flown operationally for the first time on the 28th when Wg Cdr Don Pearson photographed Tak airfield in Siam. With the surrender of the Japanese on 15 August, No 681 Sqn was employed on survey work in countries previously under enemy control. On 10 January 1946 it moved to Seletar, where PM512 was delivered to the unit that same month.

**BELOW**
Spitfire PR XIX RM632 was photographed at Benson shortly after its arrival there on 6 May 1944. The PR XIX was the last wartime PR version of the Spitfire, and it featured the powerful Griffon engine. In June 1944 RM632 was allocated to No 542 Sqn, and it was lost on 6 January 1945 when Flg Off Leslie Roberts failed to return from a sortie to Cologne (*Author's Collection*)

# INDEX